# FLY HIGH WITH
# AI

GET READY TO LAUNCH YOUR PRODUCT
MANAGEMENT CAREER IN THE AGE OF
ARTIFICIAL INTELLIGENCE

BY DIANA LEE & BALASUNDARAM SUBBUSUNDARAM

# TABLE OF CONTENTS

# Introduction:
# Navigating Product Management
# in the Age of AI

Welcome to the future of product management, where cutting-edge technology meets strategic innovation and reshapes industries faster than ever. At the core of this transformation is Artificial Intelligence (AI), a game-changer that's not just making noise—it's fundamentally changing how you, as a product manager, approach your work. This book will guide you through this new landscape, where AI isn't just a buzzword anymore—it's the driving force behind companies innovating faster, making smarter decisions, and creating products that truly revolve around you and your customers in unprecedented ways.

AI's impact on product management goes way beyond just automating tasks or crunching data. It's changing how you think about product development from the ground up, helping you reimagine value for users in ways that weren't even possible before. Whether it's Google and Amazon refining their recommendation algorithms, or Tesla pushing the limits of autonomous driving with machine learning, AI is helping companies deliver products that don't just meet customer needs—they anticipate them before anyone even realizes they exist.

According to McKinsey[1], AI is expected to add up to $13 trillion to the global economy by 2030, with early adopters seeing the biggest

---

[1] McKinsey Global Institute. "Notes from the AI frontier: Modeling the impact of AI on the world economy." September 2018. https://www.mckinsey.com/featured-

returns on investment. For you, as a product manager, this means access to insights that were unimaginable just a few years ago. AI-powered tools give you a clearer view into customer behaviors, preferences, and pain points, helping you design more personalized and engaging experiences. With advancements in natural language processing (NLP) and predictive analytics, you can now innovate faster and more precisely than ever.

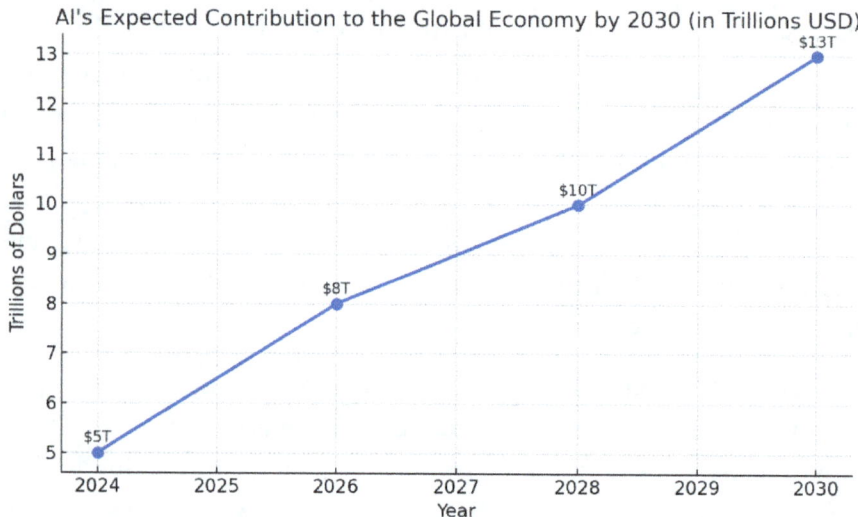

As AI keeps weaving itself into the fabric of product management, your decisions are becoming more data-driven. You no longer have to rely solely on intuition or past experience—AI lets you predict trends, simulate market reactions, and fine-tune pricing strategies. This shift makes the whole product development process more scientific and measurable.

---

insights/artificial-intelligence/notes-from-the-ai-frontier-modeling-the-impact-of-ai-on-the-world-economy

In fact, research from Harvard Business Review shows that companies using AI in their decision-making are launching products up to 20% faster, while also improving efficiency throughout their development cycles[2]. So, if you're ready to make smarter, faster choices, AI is your new best friend in product management.

However, with all this potential, there are also new challenges. Today's product managers must navigate the ethical implications of AI—addressing concerns like algorithmic bias, ensuring transparency, and maintaining trust with users. The debate surrounding AI's effects on jobs, privacy, and security is ongoing, and product managers will need to handle these concerns with care. Companies like Apple are already leading the way, prioritizing user privacy by keeping AI processing on devices instead of in the cloud, showing that it's possible to innovate responsibly.[3]

In the chapters ahead, we'll dive deep into how AI is revolutionizing product management and how you can leverage its power to stay ahead in this rapidly evolving field. Whether you're a seasoned product manager looking to sharpen your skills or someone just starting out, this book will provide the knowledge and tools you need to thrive in the age of AI.

AI is transforming not just products but the entire discipline of product management. Are you ready to embrace this change?

## 📖 Why This Matters

---

[2] Harvard Business Review. "Artificial Intelligence for the Real World." January-February 2018 issue. https://hbr.org/2018/01/artificial-intelligence-for-the-real-world

[3] Apple Inc. "Apple's Commitment to Privacy and AI." Official privacy policy and AI advancements. https://www.apple.com/newsroom/2023/06/apple-announces-powerful-new-privacy-and-security-features/

In today's hyper-competitive and fast-evolving market, innovation is no longer a luxury; it is a necessity. The ability to leverage technology, particularly artificial intelligence (AI), is a critical differentiator that separates leading companies from those struggling to keep up. For aspiring product managers and seasoned professionals alike, the ability to harness AI effectively can be the key to thriving in this new landscape. As industries across the board embrace AI, it's not just a tool—it's a force that's reshaping entire business ecosystems[4]. Understanding and adapting to AI is no longer optional but essential for those aiming to stay relevant and lead the future of product innovation.

The impact of AI on product management is profound, and its influence touches every stage of the product lifecycle. From market research and idea generation to product development, marketing, and customer feedback loops, AI is making it possible to automate, enhance, and accelerate decision-making processes that once took weeks, if not months[5]. Today, as a product manager, you've got to navigate this AI-driven world to spot opportunities, predict trends, and deliver solutions that keep up with ever-changing consumer demands. If you don't adapt, you risk falling behind, as AI is emerging quickly in business and product development.

Just look at companies like Spotify, Netflix, and Amazon—global leaders known for how they've mastered AI. For example, Spotify's ability to give you that perfectly personalized music experience isn't just about smart algorithms—it's all thanks to sophisticated AI systems that process and analyze billions of data points every single

---

[4] AI is now integrated across most major industries, transforming how businesses operate and innovate.

[5] McKinsey & Company's research reveals that companies using AI across multiple functions are already achieving higher growth rates.

day[6]. Spotify doesn't just guess what you might like to listen to next; it analyzes your listening habits in real-time, drawing from your previous behavior, preferences, and even the time of day to deliver tailored recommendations. This AI-driven personalization keeps users engaged, helping Spotify retain a loyal user base and significantly driving customer retention and long-term growth.

For you as a product manager, AI is more than just a way to improve user experience—it's a game-changer that unlocks deeper insights into how customers behave[7]. With AI, you can make smarter, data-backed decisions, helping you understand your users' pain points better, optimize features, and keep evolving your product to stay ahead of the competition.

One of the biggest advantages AI offers is the ability to predict customer needs before they even say anything. This kind of predictive insight allows your team to be proactive instead of reactive, which can be the key to leading the market rather than scrambling to catch up.

Moreover, AI empowers product managers to identify emerging trends in real-time. By analyzing vast datasets from various sources—social media, customer reviews, sales reports, and more—AI can detect patterns and shifts in customer sentiment, industry dynamics, and competitive behavior. This real-time intelligence enables product managers to stay agile, quickly iterating on their products to better serve their target audience and respond to changes in market conditions. In a world where consumer expectations are

---

[6] Spotify processes data from over 200 million active users to personalize its music recommendations.

[7] Gartner predicts that AI will be a mainstream productivity tool in product management within the next few years.

continuously evolving, the ability to pivot swiftly and make informed, data-driven decisions is invaluable.

Beyond customer insights, AI is also transforming the product development process itself. Traditionally, product teams relied on trial and error to optimize features and functions. Today, AI allows for the simulation of various scenarios, testing different product configurations in virtual environments before they are even built. This reduces time-to-market, cuts down on costs, and minimizes risk. AI also streamlines operational workflows by automating mundane tasks such as data collection and reporting, allowing product managers to focus on high-impact activities that drive innovation.

Another powerful aspect of AI in product management is its ability to personalize marketing efforts. AI-powered marketing tools enable product managers to deliver the right message to the right person at the right time. Personalized communication can dramatically increase conversion rates and customer engagement. This is a pivotal shift from the mass marketing strategies of the past, offering a more intimate and tailored customer experience that leads to greater loyalty and lifetime value.

In this book, we will take you on a comprehensive journey through the world of AI as it relates to product management. We will explore everything from the foundational concepts of AI to advanced strategies for integrating AI into every facet of your product lifecycle. You'll learn how to work effectively with AI tools and systems, and understand how to apply AI-driven insights to create products that resonate with your audience and stand out in competitive markets.

By the end of this book, you will not only have a deep understanding of how AI is reshaping the field of product management, but you will also possess the skills and knowledge to leverage AI in ways that set you apart. Whether you are just starting your career or are already leading product teams, mastering AI will be a key component of your ability to innovate and succeed. AI is not just transforming how we build products—it is redefining what is possible in product management, offering unprecedented opportunities to create smarter, more responsive, and more personalized products that delight customers and drive business success.

# PART 1:

## MASTERING THE FUNDAMENTALS OF PRODUCT MANAGEMENT

# CHAPTER 1:
# UNDERSTANDING THE
# CORE RESPONSIBILITIES OF
# A PRODUCT MANAGER

In today's fast-paced business world, your role as a product manager (PM) is more important than ever. While the core principles of product management haven't changed, the tools, strategies, and methods you use are evolving quickly—especially with AI shaking things up. As AI continues to reshape industries, you've got to not only master your core skills but also learn how to harness these new advancements. That's how you'll create innovative, competitive products that truly stand out in the market.

## 📖 The Evolving Role of a Product Manager

At its essence, product management revolves around being the linchpin that connects multiple teams—engineering, marketing, sales, customer success, and beyond. The PM's role is to guide these diverse stakeholders in working toward a common goal: delivering a product that meets customer needs while achieving business objectives. To navigate this multifaceted position, PMs must possess a deep understanding of the customer's pain points, the competitive landscape, and the company's long-term vision.

A product manager is responsible for overseeing the entire lifecycle of a product, from ideation to launch and beyond. They define the product vision, create the roadmap, prioritize features, and ensure the product evolves based on user feedback and market shifts. While the role may sound straightforward, it involves a delicate balance of strategy, execution, and communication across all stages of product development. A successful PM ensures that every team is aligned with the product's goals and that any decisions made are based on data-driven insights, customer feedback, and business metrics.

## 📖 Core Responsibilities of a Product Manager

To excel in this role, PMs must be highly skilled across several key areas, each of which plays a crucial part in the product's success:

## 1.    *Market Research and Customer Understanding*

At the heart of product management lies an in-depth understanding of customer needs and market dynamics. PMs must stay informed about the latest trends, shifts in consumer behavior, and emerging competitors. This involves conducting thorough market research, analyzing customer feedback, and collaborating with the sales and support teams to gather real-world insights. Understanding the customer's pain points allows PMs to build products that not only solve problems but deliver meaningful value.

> 🔍 *Example:* When Netflix decided to expand globally, its product management team conducted thorough market research to understand local preferences in different countries. For example, in India, Netflix realized that mobile users dominated the market, so it launched a mobile-only subscription plan. This plan was priced lower to fit local spending habits, based on extensive research into the Indian audience's preferences. By focusing on customer needs and localizing the product offering, Netflix successfully grew its user base in a new and highly competitive market[8].

## 2.    *Strategic Thinking and Product Vision*

A strong product vision is essential for guiding long-term decisions and maintaining a product's competitive edge. Product managers must define this vision by considering both the company's business goals and the ever-evolving market landscape. This requires balancing short-term priorities with long-term strategy, ensuring

---

[8] Source: Sundararajan, Sukanya. "Netflix's Mobile-Only Plan for India: A Strategic Move to Tap into the Price-Sensitive Market." Business Standard, July 2020.

that every step of the product development aligns with a broader plan for sustainable growth. Developing a clear, data-informed roadmap is essential, as it helps keep teams focused on the most impactful features and updates.

> 🔍 ***Example****:* When Elon Musk and Tesla launched the Tesla Roadster, it wasn't simply a short-term goal to build a luxury electric vehicle. Musk's vision was to create a product roadmap that would eventually lead to affordable, mass-market electric vehicles, like the Tesla Model 3. By defining a long-term strategy, Tesla was able to position itself as a leader in the electric car industry. Musk's vision involved starting with high-end electric cars to build credibility and funding, which would then allow Tesla to scale down to more affordable models and revolutionize the automotive industry[9].

## 3.    *Cross-Functional Collaboration*

One of the most challenging aspects of being a product manager is fostering collaboration across different teams. Each department—engineering, marketing, design, sales, and customer support—has its own priorities and KPIs. The PM must align these disparate teams to work toward a common goal, mediating between technical feasibility, customer desirability, and business viability. This requires strong interpersonal skills and the ability to manage

---

[9] Here's a reference for Elon Musk's long-term strategy involving Tesla. Musk's approach was detailed in his "Master Plan," which focused on initially building expensive, high-performance vehicles like the Tesla Roadster to establish credibility and generate revenue. This strategy was pivotal in funding the development of more affordable mass-market vehicles, such as the Model 3.
https://www.tesla.com/blog/master-plan-part-3

conflicts while keeping everyone focused on delivering the best possible product.

🔍 *Example:* In the development of Apple's iPhone, product managers had to align multiple departments including hardware engineering, software design, marketing, and operations. Steve Jobs himself acted as a PM, guiding teams across different functions. For instance, the engineering team needed to create a powerful and compact battery to support the software and user interface teams' requirements for a smooth, feature-rich experience. By fostering cross-functional collaboration, Apple was able to synchronize efforts and deliver a groundbreaking product that satisfied all aspects of design, usability, and performance[10].

## 4.    *Feature Prioritization and Roadmapping*

Given that resources are often limited, product managers must be adept at prioritizing features based on customer needs, technical constraints, and business value. Roadmapping is one of the core responsibilities of a PM, as it ensures that the development process follows a structured plan with clearly defined milestones. PMs must balance short-term wins (such as bug fixes and quick updates) with long-term goals (such as launching innovative features), ensuring that the product continues to evolve in a way that delivers maximum value.

🔍 *Example:* Spotify's success has been built on its ability to consistently innovate while maintaining a clear roadmap for future features. Early on, the Spotify PM team

---

[10] https://hbr.org/2020/11/how-apple-is-organized-for-innovation

prioritized features such as "Discover Weekly," which used data to provide personalized playlists for users. The team analyzed user behavior and feedback, identifying this feature as a high-impact addition that would increase user engagement. Despite many potential ideas for new features, they prioritized this one based on data, leading to high customer satisfaction and increased loyalty[11].

## 5.    *Data-Driven Decision-Making*

Modern product management is increasingly reliant on data to guide decision-making. Product managers must be comfortable working with both quantitative and qualitative data to measure the success of their products and identify areas for improvement. This includes monitoring key performance indicators (KPIs) such as user engagement, customer satisfaction, and revenue growth. AI tools have further revolutionized this aspect by providing real-time insights and predictive analytics, enabling PMs to make smarter, more informed decisions.

🔍 *Example:* Airbnb's product managers rely heavily on data to improve the user experience and adjust product features. For instance, Airbnb found that users were more likely to book properties with clearer *and* more detailed descriptions. By analyzing booking data and A/B testing various property description formats, the company refined how listings appeared in search results. This small but impactful change, based on data insights, resulted in higher booking rates and overall customer satisfaction. The PMs used data to inform their decision to make the change,

---

[11] https://www.theproductfolks.com/product-management-blog/how-spotify-became-1-music-streaming-platform-product-case-study

leading to a better user experience and increased revenue for hosts[12].

# 📖 The Evolving Role of Product Managers as AI Integration Expands

As AI becomes more integrated into the world of product management, the role of Product Managers (PMs) is evolving in exciting ways. AI-powered tools are shaking things up, making it easier for PMs to gather data, predict customer behavior, and even automate the everyday, routine tasks that used to eat up their time. With AI taking care of the heavy lifting, PMs can now spend more time focusing on strategy, innovation, and creative problem-solving.

Here's how AI is changing the game and redefining what it means to be a PM today!

## 1. *Enhanced Market Research with AI-Driven Insights*

AI tools can analyze vast datasets, providing PMs with deeper insights into customer behavior, market trends, and competitor strategies. These tools can track patterns and predict future trends with greater accuracy than traditional methods. This allows PMs to make more informed decisions about product features, pricing strategies, and market positioning, all while reducing the time spent on manual analysis.

---

[12] https://www.theproductfolks.com/product-management-case-studies/what-key-metrics-would-you-look-at-as-a-product-manager-for-airbnbs-booking-system

***How it works now:*** AI tools can analyze vast datasets to give deeper insights into customer behavior, market trends, and competitor strategies, leading to more informed decisions.

***Enhancements:***

- **Incorporate Human-Centric Validation**: While AI provides highly accurate predictive insights, it's important to combine this with human intuition and qualitative research. AI-driven insights can miss context that only direct customer interviews or surveys can provide. Product managers should complement AI analysis with qualitative feedback from focus groups, interviews, or direct user interactions to ensure the data aligns with real customer pain points.

- **Regularly Update AI Models**: AI models must be frequently updated to reflect evolving customer behaviors. Establish a feedback loop where data inputs are refined based on recent trends, seasonality, and external factors such as market disruptions (e.g., economic changes or new regulations).

## 2.   *Smarter Roadmapping and Feature Prioritization*

AI-driven analytics tools can help PMs prioritize features more effectively by predicting which updates or changes are most likely to resonate with users. This is done through advanced algorithms that analyze historical data and user behavior, allowing PMs to focus their efforts on initiatives with the highest potential impact. By leveraging AI, PMs can ensure their product roadmap is not only customer-centric but also grounded in solid data and predictive insights.

***How it works now***: AI-driven tools help PMs prioritize features by predicting the impact of certain changes or updates, ensuring that product roadmaps are data-informed.

***Enhancements:***

- **Introduce Multi-Scenario Planning**: Instead of relying solely on a single AI-based prediction for prioritization, PMs should use AI to run multiple "what-if" scenarios. This approach allows for a more flexible and adaptable roadmap that considers various potential market conditions or customer reactions.

- **Leverage Collaborative AI Platforms**: Use AI tools that allow input from all relevant stakeholders (engineering, marketing, sales). This enables more cross-functional buy-in for the roadmap, ensuring that all departments understand the reasoning behind feature prioritization and timelines.

## 3. *AI-Powered Personalization*

Personalization is becoming a key differentiator in the marketplace, and AI enables PMs to deliver highly tailored experiences. AI algorithms can segment users based on behavior, preferences, and demographics, enabling PMs to create products that offer unique value to different user groups. This personalized approach not only increases user satisfaction but also boosts customer retention and drives long-term loyalty.

***How it works now:*** AI enables PMs to offer highly tailored experiences by segmenting users based on behavior, preferences, and demographics.

### Enhancements:

- **Personalization Beyond Segmentation**: While segmentation is effective, PMs can push personalization further by implementing dynamic personalization—where AI customizes the product experience for individual users in real time, rather than relying on pre-set segments. For example, using machine learning to adapt interfaces or feature recommendations based on real-time interaction can lead to a more fluid, personalized experience.

- **Transparency in AI Usage**: With growing concerns about data privacy, product managers should focus on transparency, explaining how AI is being used to personalize experiences and why specific data is collected. This could foster user trust and encourage users to opt into more personalized experiences.

## 4.  *Automation of Routine Tasks*

AI can automate routine tasks such as data analysis, reporting, and even parts of customer support through chatbots and virtual assistants. By offloading these tasks to AI-powered systems, PMs can focus more on strategic initiatives and innovation, freeing up time to work on higher-value activities such as brainstorming new product ideas, refining the product vision, and fostering team collaboration.

*How it works now*: AI automates routine tasks such as data analysis, reporting, and parts of customer support, allowing PMs to focus on strategic initiatives.

***Enhancements:***

- **Human-AI Collaboration**: Rather than fully automating tasks, adopt a hybrid approach where AI augments human decision-making. For example, instead of AI solely creating reports, product managers can review AI-generated reports and add human-driven context or action items that AI might not account for.

- **Iterate on AI Models Based on Feedback**: Constantly collect feedback from teams using AI-driven automation to refine the models. For example, customer support chatbots can improve over time through training based on user interactions and feedback from customer service agents who can provide insights into areas AI may struggle with.

# How AI Enhances Product Management

While the core responsibilities of a product manager (PM) remain consistent—defining product vision, prioritizing features, and aligning cross-functional teams—artificial intelligence (AI) is transforming the way these responsibilities are executed, offering new avenues for efficiency and innovation. AI doesn't replace the human element in product management but rather amplifies the PM's capabilities by providing deeper insights, better decision-making tools, and automation capabilities.

One powerful example of AI-driven product management is Tesla, a global leader in electric vehicles (EVs) and autonomous driving technology. Tesla integrates AI into its product development process to enhance vehicle safety, improve user experiences, and optimize operational efficiency. The company utilizes AI not just for self-driving features but also in predicting component failures, managing supply chains, and understanding customer behavior. Tesla's product managers leverage data from AI-powered systems to make informed decisions about product upgrades, autonomous driving algorithms, and new features that anticipate customer needs[13].

Tesla's vehicles continuously collect real-time data from their vast fleet, enabling the company to analyze driving patterns, road conditions, and even potential hazards. This data is processed using AI models, helping product managers and engineers quickly identify opportunities for improvement and innovation. Through over-the-air (OTA) updates, Tesla can deliver software enhancements directly to customers' vehicles, significantly speeding up the product iteration cycle and ensuring that Tesla remains at the cutting edge of both automotive and technological innovation[14].

AI empowers product managers in several ways:

## 1. *Enhanced Data Analysis*

One of the primary benefits of AI is its ability to process vast amounts of data at incredible speeds. PMs no longer have to rely solely on manual data aggregation or basic analytics tools. AI-driven analytics platforms allow product teams to sift through terabytes of data, identifying patterns and actionable insights that would be nearly impossible to detect using traditional methods. For example, Tesla analyzes real-world driving data to refine its autonomous

---

[13] Tesla's product management strategies around autonomous driving and OTA updates demonstrate the power of AI in product innovation and real-time enhancements.

[14] https://aiexpert.network/case-study-teslas-integration-of-ai-in-automotive-innovation/
https://www.restack.io/p/tesla-ai-management-answer-autonomous-vehicles-cat-ai
https://panhandlefamily.com/tesla-ai-revolution-automotive-technology.html

driving features and predict maintenance needs in advance, resulting in safer and more reliable products.

## 2. *Real-Time Experimentation*

Product managers can now test ideas, features, or UI/UX designs in real time using AI-driven A/B testing frameworks. AI helps optimize these experiments by automatically selecting user cohorts, monitoring performance, and adjusting variables to ensure the best outcomes. For example, an e-commerce platform like Amazon uses AI to constantly test different pricing strategies, product placements, and personalized recommendations to optimize customer engagement and conversion rates[15].

## 3. *Automation of Routine Tasks*

AI allows for the automation of repetitive tasks that often take up valuable time for product managers. Tasks such as generating reports, tracking customer feedback, and gathering usage metrics can be fully automated using AI tools. This enables product teams to focus more on strategic tasks like planning roadmaps, ideating features, and communicating with stakeholders. For instance, in manufacturing industries, AI-powered platforms can manage routine quality control checks and supply chain logistics, allowing PMs to focus on innovation and long-term product goals.

## 4. *Predictive Customer Insights*

AI offers a higher level of accuracy in predicting customer needs and behaviors. Through machine learning models, PMs can forecast demand trends, detect shifts in customer preferences, and even

---

[15] Amazon utilizes AI to optimize pricing, recommendations, and supply chain management, enhancing customer experience and business performance.

identify potential risks early on. This can lead to better product-market fit and more successful product launches. For example, Spotify uses AI to predict what kind of music listeners would like based on their previous interactions, resulting in highly personalized playlists and recommendations that enhance user satisfaction and retention.

## 5.    *Accelerated Innovation*

By utilizing AI to streamline decision-making, product managers can move faster in developing and iterating on their products. AI accelerates the cycle of innovation, providing quicker insights from customer data, enabling real-time feedback loops, and reducing the time it takes to bring new features to market. This kind of rapid iteration can make a significant difference in industries that require agility, such as retail or consumer electronics[16].

AI in product management is no longer just a futuristic concept; it is a reality that drives some of the most successful products and companies today. From automotive giants like Tesla to e-commerce leaders like Amazon, AI is transforming how product managers approach their work, helping them navigate an increasingly complex digital landscape while staying responsive to customer needs.

---

[16] AI-driven innovation cycles are particularly impactful in technology and consumer-facing industries, allowing rapid iteration and market responsiveness.

# What We Learnt:

- **Why your role as a PM matters:** As a Product Manager, you're the glue that holds together multiple teams— engineering, marketing, sales, customer success, and more. Your main job? Deliver a product that solves customer problems *and* hits business goals.

- **Managing a product's entire lifecycle:** From brainstorming to launch and beyond, you're the one creating the vision, prioritizing features, and making sure the product keeps evolving based on user feedback and market trends.

- **Market research = knowing your audience:** You need to understand customer pain points and what's happening in the market. This means doing deep dives into customer feedback, industry trends, and competition to build products that add real value.

- **Strategic thinking is your secret weapon:** As a PM, you need a solid vision that lines up with both company goals *and* market realities. Long-term planning = competitive edge!

- **Collaboration is key:** Aligning different teams (with their own priorities) is tough, but it's your job to make sure everyone's on the same page, working toward the same goal. Think of yourself as the ultimate team mediator.

- **Feature prioritization 101:** Not all ideas are winners. Your job is to figure out which features matter most, balancing quick wins and long-term impact, while making the best use of available resources.

- **Data-driven decisions:** You've got to be comfortable with data. Metrics like user engagement and customer satisfaction help guide your product decisions and track success. AI tools make this even easier by offering real-time insights!

- **AI is changing the game:** AI helps with everything from deep data analysis to automating boring tasks (so you can focus on the cool stuff). It makes your job as a PM more efficient and future-proof.

- **Real-world examples:** Netflix launched a mobile-only plan in India after understanding local preferences through research. Tesla's long-term vision? Start with luxury EVs, then scale down to affordable, mass-market models. Apple aligned all its teams to create the iPhone. These companies nailed it by staying focused on customer needs, innovation, and strategy.

- **AI-powered future:** Embrace AI to stay ahead of the curve! Whether it's market research, personalized user experiences, or automating tasks, AI is the ultimate tool for PMs to level up their games.

## *Looking Forward*

As you progress through the chapters ahead, you'll dive deeper into the ways artificial intelligence can be seamlessly integrated into each phase of the product management lifecycle. From ideation and market research to product development, launch, and beyond, AI offers an opportunity to not only streamline processes but also unlock new avenues for innovation. By developing the skills and strategies outlined in this book, you will position yourself to adapt effectively to the rapidly changing technological landscape. You'll gain the tools necessary to leverage AI as a powerful strategic asset, enabling you to stay ahead of industry trends and consistently deliver value in your role. Embracing this transformation will ensure that your career as a product manager remains both competitive and forward-thinking, as you drive the next wave of AI-powered products and solutions.

# PART 2:

## THE INTERSECTION OF AI AND PRODUCT MANAGEMENT

# CHAPTER 2:
## UNDERSTANDING AI AND ITS IMPACT ON BUSINESS

AI may sound complicated, but it's actually all around us—shaping the products we use every day, often in ways we don't even notice. From the apps on our phones to the devices in our homes, AI is working behind the scenes, making our experiences more personalized and efficient. If you're in product management, AI isn't just some buzzword that gets tossed around in meetings—it's a fundamental shift in how industries operate and how products are designed. The companies that leverage AI effectively are the ones setting trends and leading markets. Whether you have a technical background or not, understanding AI is crucial to staying relevant and competitive in today's fast-paced environment. As a product manager, it's no longer just about building functional products; it's about creating intelligent solutions that can learn, adapt, and evolve at a much faster pace to meet the ever-changing needs of users, delivering significantly more value to customers in ways that weren't possible before. So, getting a grip on how AI works—and how to apply it—is essential for driving innovation and creating products that truly make an impact.

# 📖 What is AI?

At its core, Artificial Intelligence (AI) is about using machines to perform tasks that typically require human intelligence—whether that's recognizing faces in a photo, understanding speech, or making complex decisions. AI might sound like something straight out of a sci-fi movie, but it's actually something we interact with on a daily basis. If you've ever used facial recognition to unlock your phone or had Google Maps suggest a faster route based on traffic, you've already experienced AI in action.

But how does it work? Two of the key concepts within AI are *machine learning* and *natural language processing* (NLP). While they may sound technical, understanding these ideas is crucial if you're diving into the world of product management and want to build AI-driven products.

## 1.  *Machine Learning: Teaching Machines to Learn*

Think of **machine learning** as the brainpower behind AI. Unlike traditional programming, where every action a computer takes is explicitly coded, machine learning allows computers to learn from data and improve their performance over time. You can think of it like training a dog—at first, you have to show the dog what you want it to do, but over time, it starts picking up on patterns and can respond without constant instructions.

> 🔍 *For example:* when you're using social media apps like Instagram or TikTok, the platform's algorithms are constantly learning from your interactions—what posts you like, how long you watch certain videos, who you follow. Over time, machine learning systems process that data and start predicting what you're most likely to engage with, curating a feed that keeps you scrolling. The more you interact, the better these systems get at guessing what content you'll enjoy, leading to a highly personalized experience.

> 🔍 Another great example of machine learning in action is in **healthcare**. Hospitals and doctors use AI-powered systems to scan through thousands of medical images, learning to detect early signs of diseases like cancer. These systems can spot patterns that even experienced professionals might miss, leading to faster and more accurate diagnoses. This isn't just improving outcomes; it's saving lives by catching diseases at an earlier, more treatable stage.

## 2.   *Natural Language Processing (NLP): Understanding Human Language*

Now, let's talk about **Natural Language Processing (NLP)**. This is the branch of AI that allows machines to understand, interpret, and respond to human language. Whether you're asking Alexa to play your favorite playlist or using Google Translate to decipher a foreign language text, you're using NLP.

But NLP is more than just responding to basic commands. In the world of customer service, for instance, many companies use AI-powered chatbots to interact with customers in real-time. Ever reached out to a company's support page and had a chatbot help you with basic questions like tracking an order or resetting a password? That's NLP at work, helping machines understand and respond to human queries.

What's even cooler is how NLP is getting more sophisticated. Some systems can now understand the context behind the words, not just the words themselves. For example, if you ask, "What's the weather like in New York next Tuesday?" the AI not only understands that you want a future weather forecast for a specific location, but it also processes that you're talking about a future date. This kind of advanced language understanding is what powers things like **virtual assistants**—whether it's Siri helping you set reminders, or customer support bots that handle queries 24/7.

NLP is also evolving to detect sentiment and tone. That means AI can now analyze whether a customer review is positive or negative without needing human intervention. Brands use this technology to gauge public opinion on social media or product reviews, helping them understand customer needs and preferences better.

# 📖 AI in Everyday Life

Now, you might be familiar with AI recommending your next Netflix show, but that's just the tip of the iceberg. AI has embedded itself into so many aspects of our lives that we often don't even notice it's there. Here are some examples beyond the obvious:

- **Smart Homes**: Smart devices like thermostats and security systems powered by AI are getting better at predicting your preferences. A smart thermostat can learn your routine—when you leave the house, when you're likely to return, and when you like your home to be cooler or warmer. This means it can adjust the temperature automatically, saving energy and making your life easier.

- **Shopping Recommendations**: Have you ever noticed how Amazon seems to know exactly what you might want to buy next? That's AI in the background, analyzing your previous purchases, browsing history, and even what other customers with similar shopping habits are buying. It then suggests products that match your preferences, streamlining the shopping experience. AI is also used in **dynamic pricing**, where online retailers adjust prices in real-time based on demand, competition, and other factors.

- **Gaming**: AI is also a major player in the gaming world. It's used to create intelligent opponents in games or adaptive environments that change based on how you play. Take a game like *The Sims*, where the characters interact with each other based on their unique personality traits and moods. AI algorithms are what make that happen, creating a dynamic gaming experience that feels unique each time.

- **Finance**: Ever gotten a notification from your bank asking if a recent transaction was really made by you? AI powers these systems to flag suspicious activity in real-time. It scans your transaction history and spending habits to detect unusual patterns, helping prevent fraud before it even happens.

### AI Isn't Perfect, But It's Evolving Fast

As exciting as all of this is, AI isn't without its limitations. AI systems are only as good as the data they are trained on. If an AI is trained on biased or incomplete data, it can make faulty or even harmful decisions. This is a big challenge in areas like facial recognition, where AI has been criticized for its inaccuracies, especially when it comes to identifying people of different ethnic backgrounds.

However, as AI continues to evolve, so do the efforts to make it more reliable, fair, and ethical. More companies and researchers are focusing on making AI transparent and explainable, ensuring that its decisions can be understood and trusted by users.

## How AI is Revolutionizing Industries

AI is shaking up just about every industry out there—from healthcare to retail to entertainment. Let's talk about a few examples:

### 1. Healthcare: Revolutionizing Diagnostics and Treatment

AI is making waves in healthcare by enabling quicker and more accurate diagnoses. For instance, AI tools can analyze medical images like X-rays, MRIs, and CT scans with remarkable precision, sometimes even outperforming human doctors in detecting diseases like cancer. Think about the potential here: faster diagnoses mean earlier treatments and better outcomes. AI also supports personalized medicine. Imagine feeding your medical history, genetic profile, and lifestyle data into an AI system, which then tailors treatment plans specifically for you—no more one-size-fits-all prescriptions.

Even in surgery, AI-driven robots like the da Vinci Surgical System are assisting surgeons in performing minimally invasive procedures with pinpoint accuracy. The future could see even more AI integration into routine check-ups, remote monitoring, and even mental health assessments.

## 2.    *Retail: Personalizing Your Shopping Experience*

Ever notice how your favorite e-commerce site seems to suggest just the right product? That's AI in action. Retailers are using machine learning algorithms to track and analyze consumer behavior—what you buy, what you browse, how long you stay on a page—to curate recommendations tailored to your tastes. But it doesn't stop there. In physical stores, AI is also transforming the shopping experience. Take Amazon, for instance: they've introduced self-checkout kiosks with computer vision technology that can identify items without barcodes, making the process faster and smoother[17].

---

[17] An example of AI-enhanced shopping can be seen at Sam's Club, a membership-based retailer owned by Walmart. They use AI-powered tools like the "Scan & Go" app, which allows customers to scan items with their phones while shopping and pay directly through the app, bypassing traditional checkout lines. Additionally, they're rolling out AI-driven "seamless exit" technology that leverages computer vision to verify cart contents without manual receipt checks, cutting down wait times by 23% at exits Walmart Global Tech Walmart Corporate Walmart Global Tech. This AI application not only enhances the in-store experience but also streamlines operations and minimizes delays, illustrating the broader role of AI in revolutionizing retail Walmart Corporate.

AI also plays a role in inventory management, reducing waste by predicting demand more accurately and ensuring that shelves are stocked with items you're likely to buy next.

## 3. Entertainment: More than Just Content Recommendations

When we talk about AI in entertainment, most people immediately think of Netflix or YouTube recommending what to watch next. But it goes deeper than that. AI is even creating content! Platforms like RunwayML and DeepArt allow artists and creators to leverage AI to generate art, videos, and even music. In gaming, AI is used to design more immersive worlds and smarter, more adaptive non-playable characters (NPCs), giving players a more realistic and dynamic gaming experience.

Even the film industry is tapping into AI to streamline the scriptwriting process and predict box office performance. ScriptBook, for example, uses AI to analyze scripts and forecast their success based on storyline elements and audience preferences.

## 4. Agriculture: Boosting Food Production

AI is not just limited to tech-heavy industries. Even agriculture is undergoing a digital transformation thanks to AI. Farmers now use AI-driven drones to monitor crop health, irrigation systems, and soil quality in real-time. AI-based predictive models can help farmers know the best times to plant and harvest, optimizing crop yield. Precision agriculture tools like John Deere's AI-powered tractors use data to make farming more efficient, reducing waste and increasing productivity—essential in a world with an ever-growing population.

## 5.  *Finance: Detecting Fraud and Automating Trading*

The finance industry has been quick to adopt AI for various purposes, from fraud detection to algorithmic trading. AI systems analyze vast amounts of financial data in real time to spot irregularities and flag potentially fraudulent transactions before they happen. Similarly, AI is revolutionizing stock market trading by making predictions based on historical data and executing trades at lightning speed. Robo-advisors like Betterment and Wealthfront are also using AI to help people manage their investments, providing personalized advice without the need for a human financial advisor.

## 6.  *Education: Personalized Learning for Everyone*

In education, AI is making learning more personalized and accessible. Platforms like Coursera, Khan Academy, and Duolingo use AI to adapt lessons to your individual learning pace. Whether you're cramming for finals or trying to learn a new language, AI algorithms can assess your strengths and weaknesses and tweak the curriculum accordingly. AI tutors and chatbots are also becoming a thing, offering 24/7 assistance for students who need extra help.

What's more, AI can help educators identify students who may be struggling and offer timely interventions, potentially reducing dropout rates and improving academic performance.

## 7.  *Transportation: Autonomous Vehicles and Smarter Logistics*

The transportation industry is another area where AI is making a big impact. Self-driving cars, like those developed by Tesla and Waymo, rely heavily on AI to interpret data from sensors and cameras, navigate roads, and make real-time decisions to avoid accidents. Beyond personal vehicles, AI is optimizing logistics and delivery services. Companies like UPS and FedEx use AI to determine the most efficient routes, saving fuel and reducing delivery times.

In public transport, AI can improve traffic flow by analyzing data from traffic cameras, sensors, and even weather patterns to optimize stoplights and reduce congestion.

## *The Takeaway: AI is Here to Stay*

From personalized healthcare and shopping experiences to smarter agriculture and autonomous vehicles, AI is reshaping industries in ways that are both fascinating and practical. This transformation opens up endless possibilities—whether you're looking to enter the job market or simply wondering how AI will make your day-to-day life easier, it's clear that AI is going to play a central role in the future.

The exciting part? We're only scratching the surface of what's possible with AI. So, whether you're fascinated by its ability to diagnose diseases or create art, one thing's for sure: AI is here to stay, and it's only getting smarter.

In each of these examples, AI is doing the heavy lifting behind the scenes, crunching data and finding patterns that humans might miss.

# 📖 How AI-Powered Products Differ from Traditional Products

Now, you might be thinking, *"Okay, cool. But what does this mean for me as a product manager?"* The big difference between AI products and traditional products is that AI-driven ones learn and adapt. This means the product is never truly "finished." It's in a constant state of improvement, much like how your phone regularly gets software updates to fix bugs or add features—except with AI, the changes are more dynamic and responsive to real-time data.

Here's how AI products are unique:

## *1.    Constant Learning Cycles:*

AI products thrive on data. They rely heavily on user interactions, feedback, and other external inputs to learn and improve. Imagine a language translation app that gets better with every use. The more users engage with it, the better it becomes at understanding complex phrases, slang, and even dialects. This constant learning is what makes AI products special—they evolve. Take Google Maps as an example. Initially, it might recommend a route based on basic factors like distance, but over time, it adjusts its recommendations based on traffic patterns, user preferences, and even environmental changes like road closures. The product is always "learning" from how it's used, making future interactions smoother and more accurate.

## *2.    Data Dependency:*

AI isn't just powered by code; it needs a steady diet of high-quality data to function optimally. As a product manager, you're no longer just focusing on the interface or functionality; you're now thinking about how to gather, clean, and feed relevant data into your AI system. Think about AI used in healthcare, for instance. Machine learning models in medical diagnostics rely on vast amounts of medical records, imaging data, and patient histories to make accurate predictions. The key challenge isn't just creating an AI model, but making sure that the data feeding it is robust, relevant, and ethically sourced.

## 3. *Designing for Both Human Users and AI Agents*

Building an AI-driven product means you're not just designing for human users anymore; you're designing for the AI agents as well. It's like creating a system where both the human and machine collaborate. Think of it as if you're designing a team—one human, one machine. The human might be your main "user," but the AI is part of that experience, too, constantly learning and adapting to better serve the human.

Take autonomous vehicles, for instance. When Tesla designs its self-driving cars, they're considering both the human driver and the car's AI system. The human might want manual control over the car in certain situations, but there are times when the AI takes the lead, such as in highway autopilot mode. The key challenge is designing a system that feels natural to the human—like they can trust the AI—but also ensures that the AI works effectively in the background without causing confusion or frustration.

In essence, you're balancing two experiences: ensuring the AI's actions feel intuitive and don't interrupt the user's flow while simultaneously giving the human enough control so they feel empowered, not overrun by the machine.

## 4.   *Ensuring Seamless Human-AI Interaction*

Seamless interaction is the secret sauce of a great AI product. If your product's AI feels clunky, confusing, or frustrating, users will bail fast. Gen Z, especially, has little patience for poorly designed digital experiences. The best AI feels invisible—it should work quietly in the background while the user enjoys a smooth, uninterrupted experience.

A good example of this is recommendation algorithms on platforms like YouTube. Every time you watch a video, the AI silently takes note of your preferences—how long you watch, what topics you prefer, what you skip—and it serves up content tailored specifically for you. The AI is in the background doing all the heavy lifting, but as a user, you don't even notice it; you just enjoy a personalized experience.

Now let's compare this to AI in smart home devices, like the Nest thermostat. The thermostat learns your temperature preferences over time and automatically adjusts to them. In the beginning, you might manually set the temperature throughout the day, but over time, the AI learns when you typically come home, what temperature you prefer at night, and it adjusts accordingly. It's seamless, making your life easier without you having to think about it.

But here's the catch: not all AI products are smooth. Imagine you're talking to a voice assistant like Alexa, and it constantly misinterprets your requests. If this keeps happening, you'd stop using it. The same is true for AI-powered customer service bots. If a bot can't resolve a customer's issue quickly or fails to recognize when it should hand off to a human, that's a failure in human-AI interaction. Users don't care how "advanced" the AI is; they care about whether it works smoothly for them.

# ☐ Practical Tips for Managing AI Products

As a product manager, you're in charge of making sure the AI product you're working on creates value for users, not headaches. Here are some key takeaways:

- **Understand your data pipeline:** The quality of your AI depends on the quality of data it receives. Make sure you have a strong strategy in place for gathering and refining data inputs. If you're working on an AI product for e-commerce, for example, ensure that the customer data is clean, privacy-protected, and valuable for generating meaningful insights.

- **Focus on user experience, not just AI performance:** Just because your AI can predict something with 99% accuracy doesn't mean users will love it. The AI's actions need to fit naturally within the user experience. Pay attention to how the AI integrates into your product's overall flow and whether it adds value without disrupting the user.

- **Build trust:** AI can sometimes feel "too smart" for comfort, especially when it comes to decisions like financial recommendations or healthcare diagnostics. It's your job as a product manager to ensure that users understand the AI's role and feel confident in its recommendations or actions.

# ✦ Case Studies: AI-Driven Products

Let's look at some practical, real-world case studies of AI-driven products that go beyond typical examples like Netflix or Spotify. These examples will highlight how AI is reshaping industries and offer valuable lessons for product managers.

## 1. *AI-Powered Healthcare: IBM Watson Health*

**Overview:**

IBM's Watson Health is a leader in leveraging AI for medical diagnostics and treatment. Watson uses AI to sift through massive amounts of medical data, including patient records, clinical research, and real-time data inputs like lab results or scans. It assists doctors by providing treatment options based on the latest research and the patient's specific health data.

**AI in Action:**

One of Watson's biggest use cases is in oncology (cancer treatment). Doctors use Watson to analyze cancer patients' genetic profiles and medical histories, allowing them to identify potential treatments faster and with more precision. By doing so, Watson helps doctors personalize care plans and even flag potential drug interactions or adverse effects.

**Why It's Relevant for Product Managers:**

This example showcases how AI can deliver personalized, data-driven solutions that empower professionals (in this case, doctors) to make better decisions. As a product manager, it's your role to ensure the AI product is user-friendly, transparent, and trustworthy. One of the challenges IBM faced was getting doctors to trust AI recommendations, so they had to work closely with the medical community to fine-tune the product's output to match real-world clinical needs. The lesson? No matter how advanced your AI product is, collaboration with end users is critical to ensure adoption.

## 2. *Duolingo: AI-Driven Personalized Learning*

**Overview:**

Duolingo, a popular language-learning app, uses AI to tailor lessons based on individual user performance. The AI tracks each user's progress, identifying areas of strength and weakness, and adapts the learning path in real-time to meet their needs. If a user struggles with a particular grammar rule, for example, the app serves more practice on that rule, while advancing users who master a topic quickly to more challenging content.

**AI in Action:**

Duolingo's AI system dynamically adjusts the difficulty of exercises based on the learner's interaction history. It even predicts how likely a user is to forget a word and prompts them to review it at just the right time to reinforce memory. Additionally, AI-generated feedback helps users improve pronunciation and grammar.

**Why It's Relevant for Product Managers:**

Duolingo demonstrates how AI can create a personalized and adaptive learning experience. The challenge for product managers is balancing AI personalization with user motivation. Duolingo does this by gamifying the learning process—incorporating leaderboards, streaks, and rewards. For product managers, the takeaway here is that AI alone isn't enough. You also need to create a compelling user experience that keeps people engaged long-term.

## 3. *Tesla's Autopilot: AI in Autonomous Driving*

**Overview:**

Tesla's Autopilot is one of the most well-known applications of AI in the automotive industry. The system uses deep learning to interpret data from cameras, sensors, and radar to make real-time driving decisions. Tesla's AI allows cars to navigate highways, change lanes, and even park autonomously.

**AI in Action:**

The system continuously learns from the data of millions of Tesla vehicles on the road. This allows Autopilot to improve its driving algorithms over time, becoming better at identifying road hazards, interpreting road signs, and navigating difficult conditions like rain or snow. The cars use this collective data to enhance their self-driving capabilities through over-the-air updates.

**Why It's Relevant for Product Managers:**

Tesla's Autopilot shows the power of AI to create life-altering products, but it also highlights the importance of managing user expectations. While Tesla's AI is incredibly advanced, it's not perfect, and the company has faced legal challenges when users mistakenly believed Autopilot was fully autonomous. Product managers need to focus on clear communication, ensuring users understand the limitations of AI while still delivering innovation.

## 4.    *H&M: AI-Powered Supply Chain Optimization*

**Overview:**

H&M, a global fashion retailer, uses AI to optimize its supply chain. The company employs machine learning to analyze factors like weather patterns, past sales data, and customer preferences to predict future demand. This helps H&M make smarter decisions about inventory management, ensuring stores are stocked with the right items at the right time.

**AI in Action:**

The AI-driven system allows H&M to forecast trends and manage inventory levels more efficiently. For example, it can predict which styles will be popular in certain regions based on past sales patterns and even optimize logistics to reduce waste. This level of insight helps the company avoid overproduction, reducing costs and minimizing its environmental footprint.

**Why It's Relevant for Product Managers:**

For product managers, H&M's approach[18] shows how AI can enhance operational efficiency, not just customer-facing products. The lesson here is the importance of integrating AI solutions across different aspects of your business—not just product features, but also behind-the-scenes processes like supply chain management. As a product manager, understanding how AI can improve the whole value chain is critical to delivering a better product and experience.

---

[18] For more on H&M's use of AI in supply chain management, see Analytics India Magazine.

## *5.    Grammarly: AI-Powered Writing Assistant*

### Overview:

Grammarly is an AI-powered writing tool that helps users improve their grammar, spelling, tone, and clarity. What sets Grammarly apart is its ability to understand context and provide advanced suggestions[19], not just for correcting errors but also for improving writing style based on the audience or intent.

### AI in Action:

Grammarly uses machine learning models trained on a vast dataset of text to offer real-time suggestions. It learns from a user's writing patterns and can provide tailored advice. For instance, it recognizes if a user is writing a formal email versus a casual social media post and adjusts its tone recommendations accordingly.

### Why It's Relevant for Product Managers:

Grammarly's success lies in how well its AI aligns with user needs. It's not just about correcting grammar—it's about understanding the context of each writing situation. This is a key takeaway for product managers: ensure that your AI solves real user problems and fits naturally into their workflows. In Grammarly's case, the product integrates seamlessly into platforms like Microsoft Word and Google Docs, making it easy to use across multiple writing environments.

---

[19] For more information on how Grammarly uses AI to enhance grammar, tone, and writing style based on context, visit Grammarly's official site
Grammarly: Free AI Writing Assistance

## 6. *Stitch Fix: AI-Driven Fashion Recommendations*

**Overview:**

Stitch Fix is an online personal styling service that uses AI to recommend clothing items based on a customer's style preferences, size, and feedback. The AI analyzes user data and combines it with feedback from human stylists to curate personalized fashion "fixes" for each customer.

**AI in Action:**

Stitch Fix's AI takes into account data points such as past purchases, style preferences, and even social media behavior to deliver personalized clothing recommendations. Customers receive a box of curated items (the "fix"), and they can keep what they like and return the rest. AI also learns from returned items to fine-tune future recommendations, creating a more personalized experience over time.

**Why It's Relevant for Product Managers:**

Stitch Fix highlights the power of combining AI with human expertise. While the AI makes initial recommendations, human stylists review and refine those suggestions, creating a unique hybrid approach. For product managers, this shows the value of using AI to augment human decision-making rather than replace it entirely. It's about finding the right balance between automation and human touch.

# 📖 Conclusion

These case studies show how AI is transforming industries from healthcare to fashion. As a product manager, your job is not just to understand how AI works but how to integrate it in ways that genuinely enhance the user experience. Whether it's improving operational efficiency, personalizing products, or delivering cutting-edge features, AI is the tool that can take your product to the next level. The future is here, and as a product manager, you're at the forefront of driving that innovation forward.

---

 **What We Learnt:**

- **AI is Everywhere:** AI is already a big part of our everyday lives, from smart devices to apps, even though we might not always notice it.

- **AI is Crucial for Product Managers:** It's not just a tech buzzword—AI is fundamentally changing how industries operate and how products are designed. If you're a product manager, understanding AI is essential to staying competitive and relevant.

- **Machine Learning Powers AI:** Machine learning is what allows AI to learn from data and improve over time—think of Instagram or TikTok predicting what you want to see next.

- **NLP (Natural Language Processing) Makes AI Understand Us:** This is the part of AI that enables machines to understand and respond to human language, like when you talk to Alexa or use a chatbot for customer service.

- **AI Products Never Stop Improving:** AI-driven products evolve constantly based on user interactions and data. Unlike traditional products, they're always learning and adapting— Google Maps getting smarter with traffic data is a good example.

- **Data is Key:** AI relies heavily on data to function. As a product manager, your role includes ensuring that the data feeding your AI system is clean, relevant, and ethical.

- **Designing for Humans and AI:** When building AI products, you're designing for both the human user and the AI itself. It's about balancing human control with AI's autonomous features—like Tesla's Autopilot.

- **Human-AI Interaction Must Be Seamless:** If the AI is clunky or confusing, users will quickly abandon it. The best AI feels invisible, working in the background to enhance the user experience—think YouTube recommendations or Nest smart thermostats.

- **Case Studies Highlight AI's Potential:** From IBM Watson revolutionizing healthcare to Stitch Fix's AI-powered fashion recommendations, real-world examples show how AI is transforming industries.

- **Key Takeaway for Product Managers:** Whether you're building a customer-facing product or optimizing back-end processes, AI is the tool that can help you drive innovation and create more impactful, personalized experiences for users.

# CHAPTER 3:
## AI AND ETHICAL PRODUCT MANAGEMENT

When you're building products with AI, one of the biggest challenges you'll face is balancing innovation with responsibility. It's exciting to create something groundbreaking, but if you don't consider the ethical implications, things can go south—fast. The power AI holds is immense, and with great power comes great responsibility (yes, I'm quoting Spiderman here, but it fits). So, let's talk about how you can be responsible with AI and why it matters.

# 📖 Challenges and Best Practices of Responsible AI

The first thing to know is that AI isn't neutral. It's only as good as the data it's trained on, and that data comes with biases, gaps, and sometimes even errors. Imagine creating a product designed to help people find jobs, but because the AI was trained on biased data, it ends up favoring certain demographics over others. Not cool, right?

## *Challenge 1: Bias in AI*

AI systems are inherently tied to the data they're trained on, and if that data reflects human biases, the AI will too. For instance, Amazon scrapped an AI recruiting tool after it was found to be biased against women. The system had been trained on resumes submitted to the company over a 10-year period, which predominantly came from men, leading the AI to favor male candidates over equally qualified female ones. This isn't just a theoretical problem; it has real-world consequences that affect people's lives and opportunities.

**Best Practice:** One of the most effective ways to combat bias is by building diverse teams. A study by McKinsey[20] shows that companies with greater diversity in their workforce are more likely to outperform their peers financially. When different backgrounds and experiences are involved in the creation of AI, potential biases can be spotted early on. Another best practice is continuous monitoring—AI isn't static. Regular audits of your AI systems are crucial, especially as societal norms and expectations shift over time.

---

[20] https://www.mckinsey.com/capabilities/people-and-organizational-performance/our-insights/is-there-a-payoff-from-top-team-diversity

**Q** *Example*: Google, after facing criticism for bias in its AI algorithms, implemented a Responsible AI team dedicated to researching and developing ways to reduce bias and improve fairness across all its AI products. They also launched tools like the "What-If Tool," which helps developers visualize how changes in input data can impact the behavior of machine learning models.

## Challenge 2: Transparency *(The Black Box Problem)*

Many AI models, particularly deep learning ones, function like a "black box"—you provide input, something happens inside the model, and then an output appears. But why did the AI make a particular decision? This lack of transparency can cause trust issues, especially in high-stakes situations like healthcare or finance. For instance, if an AI system recommends denying a loan application, the applicant deserves to know why.

**Best Practice:** Transparency is key to trust. A good practice is to use "explainable AI" (XAI), which allows users to understand how and why the AI makes decisions. Companies should document how the model was built, what data was used, and the rationale behind key decisions. This isn't just a technical issue; it's also about building a relationship of trust with customers and regulators.

**Q** *Example*: The European Union's General Data Protection Regulation (GDPR) mandates that users have the "right to explanation" when decisions are made using AI. This has pushed companies to focus on more transparent algorithms. IBM, for example, has invested heavily in explainable AI to ensure its models can be trusted and understood by its users.

## *Challenge 3: Accountability*

When AI goes wrong, who takes the blame? This is especially important when the AI is used in sensitive areas like content moderation, autonomous vehicles, or healthcare diagnostics. If an AI misdiagnoses a patient or causes an accident, who is responsible? It's not enough to say "the AI made a mistake"—there needs to be a clear line of accountability.

**Best Practice:** From the outset, companies should establish responsibility for AI decisions. This might involve setting up internal governance structures that oversee the use of AI across all projects. Many organizations now have a Chief AI Ethics Officer to manage these risks. Additionally, companies should be proactive about implementing ethical AI frameworks that ensure responsibility doesn't get passed around in circles.

> **Example:** Tesla's autonomous driving features have faced scrutiny when accidents occur, with debates over whether the blame lies with the company, the driver, or the technology. Tesla, in response, has built-in safeguards requiring drivers to keep their hands on the wheel, reminding them that they're ultimately responsible even when the car is in autopilot mode. This is an example of how accountability can be shared between human operators and AI systems, but companies must still take ownership of the technology they deploy.

## *Challenge 4: AI and Job Displacement*

The automation of jobs through AI can lead to large-scale displacement of workers. For example, companies in manufacturing, logistics, and customer service have increasingly turned to AI-driven automation, reducing the need for human labor.

A study by the McKinsey Global Institute estimates that by 2030, automation could displace as many as 400 million workers globally[21].

**Best Practice:** Invest in upskilling and reskilling your workforce. Companies like AT&T have created extensive reskilling programs to help employees transition to roles that require human creativity and complex problem-solving, areas where AI currently struggles.

> 🔍 *Example*: AT&T's Future Ready program offers training in areas such as AI, data science, and cybersecurity, helping its employees pivot to higher-skilled jobs rather than being displaced .

Additionally, governments and companies need to collaborate to develop safety nets and new educational initiatives for workers displaced by automation. This includes public-private partnerships that fund retraining programs and policies like universal basic income (UBI) to support individuals in transition periods.

## 📖 Ensuring Accuracy, Compliance, and Accountability in Product Design

As AI continues to evolve, so does the regulatory landscape. It's not enough to just build a cool product—you have to make sure it's accurate, compliant, and accountable. That means you need to ensure that your AI delivers the right results and does so ethically.

---

[21] https://www.mckinsey.com/featured-insights/future-of-work/jobs-lost-jobs-gained-what-the-future-of-work-will-mean-for-jobs-skills-and-wages

## 1.    *Ensuring Accuracy in AI*

Accuracy isn't just a nice-to-have; it's a **must-have** when it comes to AI-driven products. Think of it like this: AI is making decisions that affect real people. Whether it's recommending a song, diagnosing a medical condition, or navigating a car, the stakes are high. If your AI isn't accurate, it's not just a technical fail—it's a trust issue.

Take healthcare AI, for example. Imagine an AI diagnosing a disease but missing the correct diagnosis because the training data wasn't broad enough or the algorithm wasn't updated. This could lead to life-threatening outcomes. Or think about a self-driving car. A glitch in decision-making on the road isn't just a technical bug— it could mean someone's safety.

So, how do you ensure accuracy? Here's where **continuous validation and testing** come in. AI models can degrade over time, especially as new data is introduced or contexts change. You need to test your AI systems regularly, in real-world settings. A famous example of this is Tesla's self-driving AI, which constantly collects and updates data from every car on the road to improve its accuracy and decision-making. You don't want to just set it and forget it— you've got to be proactive in updating, retraining, and improving your models.

📌 *Pro Tip:* You can implement **A/B testing** with live users to assess the performance of your AI in different environments. Just like how Instagram tests new features with a small group of users before rolling it out globally, you can pilot your AI models in controlled environments to gather insights.

## 2.   *Compliance in the Age of AI*

Let's talk compliance—it might not sound flashy, but it's critical, especially when working with AI. Different regions have different laws governing AI use, and these laws can evolve quickly. For example, **Europe's General Data Protection Regulation (GDPR)** has made waves worldwide by imposing strict rules on data privacy. If your product handles personal data, you need to make sure you're compliant not only to avoid fines (which can be huge!) but also to build **trust** with your users.

Think of how platforms like TikTok or Instagram handle your data. Users are increasingly aware of how their information is being used, and any hint of misuse can damage your brand's reputation. If your AI product is global, you'll need to navigate different legal environments—what's cool in the U.S. might not fly in Europe or Asia.

Here's a concrete example: **Apple's privacy policies**. Apple took a strong stance on privacy with its App Tracking Transparency feature, giving users more control over who can track their data. This shift not only kept them compliant with evolving privacy laws but also helped them build trust with users who value data security.

📌 *Pro Tip*: Hire a compliance officer or partner with legal experts to ensure you're up to date with the latest AI regulations. This way, your product won't just be innovative—it'll be legally sound, too.

## 3.   *Building Accountability Into AI Product Design*

Finally, let's talk about accountability. Accountability is about making sure that if something goes wrong, there's a clear plan and team in place to fix it. In AI, things can and do go wrong—just ask

Facebook, which had issues with its AI content moderation system flagging the wrong posts or letting harmful content slip through.

So, how do you build accountability? **Clear roles and responsibilities** are a great place to start. Make sure your team knows who is responsible for each part of the AI system, from design to deployment. If a user reports an issue—let's say an AI assistant is giving wrong information—who's going to fix it? Having clear feedback loops where users can report problems and get quick fixes is key.

Think about Spotify's recommendation algorithm. If users are unhappy with their suggestions, they can provide feedback, and the algorithm is retrained to improve. This continuous feedback loop ensures the AI is always learning and evolving, while users feel like they have a voice.

> ✦ *Pro Tip*: Establish an **AI ethics board** or create internal accountability committees that review AI decisions regularly. Companies like Google and Microsoft have introduced ethics boards to review and guide the development of their AI systems to avoid any unintended biases or issues.

## *Bringing It All Together*

Ensuring **accuracy**, staying **compliant**, and building **accountability** are the trifecta of successful AI product design. But it's not just about following rules—it's about doing right by your users. Gen Z, in particular, values brands and products that are transparent, ethical, and trustworthy. They care deeply about how

AI is used, and they want to know that companies are prioritizing their safety and privacy.

So, whether you're developing the next cool AI-powered app or working on a more serious use case like healthcare, keep these principles in mind. Accuracy isn't just technical—it's about trust. Compliance isn't just legal—it's about building a product users feel safe using. And accountability? That's what keeps users coming back because they know you've got their back.

By focusing on these pillars, you'll not only build better products—you'll build products that people actually **want** to use.

# 📖 AI and Data Privacy: Navigating Regulatory Landscapes

Let's face it—AI is changing the world, but with that comes the massive issue of data privacy. Nowadays, users (like you and me) are hyper-aware of where our data is going, who's using it, and how it's being stored. The good news? Companies are getting better at this, but the bad news? It's also getting complicated, thanks to global privacy laws that are evolving fast.

This isn't just about protecting users; it's about staying on top of a *huge* web of regulations. Messing this up can be costly, both in terms of fines and lost trust. So, let's break it down.

## *Understanding Regulatory Frameworks*

Depending on where you're operating, the laws you need to follow might be totally different. And yeah, that can be confusing. Let's go through some of the big ones:

- **GDPR (General Data Protection Regulation)**: This is the European Union's data privacy law, which gives users a ton of control over their personal data. If your product has even a single user in Europe, you've gotta comply with GDPR. It's all about consent, transparency, and giving users the right to be "forgotten" (i.e., delete their data when they want).

- **CCPA (California Consumer Privacy Act)**: In the U.S., there isn't a national law (yet), but states are taking matters into their own hands. California leads the charge with the CCPA, which gives Californians the right to know what data is being collected, how it's being used, and to request its deletion. Think of it as the American cousin of GDPR.

🔍 *Example*: In 2020, TikTok faced scrutiny and fines for violating CCPA and COPPA (Children's Online Privacy Protection Act) by allegedly collecting data on minors without proper consent. This led to changes in how the app handles user data, showing how serious privacy laws are getting.

## ⚙ Best Practices for Data Privacy

Now that you know the legal side, how do you actually apply this to your AI-driven product? Here are some strategies to not only keep regulators happy but also earn your users' trust:

### 1. *Data Minimization*

When it comes to data collection, less is more. Collect only what you need for your app or product to work. If you're developing an AI-driven fitness app, you probably don't need your users' home addresses or social security numbers—just data about their fitness routines, diet, and progress.

🔍 *Example*: Apple is a leader in data minimization. Apple Health, for instance, keeps health data on the device instead of storing it in the cloud unless users explicitly consent. This helps users feel more in control of their sensitive info.

## 2.    *Anonymization*

Data anonymization is key to protecting users' privacy. This means stripping data of personal identifiers so that even if someone does hack into it, they can't trace it back to an individual.

🔍 *Example*: Spotify does this well. When collecting data to improve song recommendations, they remove personal identifiers, meaning even if someone sees the data, they can't tell it's you who's been listening to those throwback 2000s hits.

## 3.    *User Control*

Users want to feel in charge of their own data. They should be able to access, edit, or delete their personal information whenever they want—without jumping through hoops.

🔍 *Example*: Instagram gives users easy control over their data. You can download your data or delete your account in just a few clicks, making it transparent and easy to manage.

## 4.   *Security*

Strong security measures are non-negotiable when you're handling personal data. This includes encryption (turning data into unreadable code), secure data storage, and regular security audits.

🔍 *Example*: WhatsApp uses end-to-end encryption to ensure that your messages are secure and can't be accessed by anyone—not even WhatsApp itself.

## 📖 What Happens if You Don't Comply with Data Privacy Laws?

Let's face it: handling data properly is no longer just "nice to have." It's a non-negotiable. With governments worldwide tightening up data privacy laws, companies—big or small—must comply. Ignoring these regulations isn't just a slap on the wrist. It can lead to hefty fines, losing your customers' trust, or even being banned from selling your product in certain regions. Scary, right?

But don't worry. Let's dive into what this all means for you and how companies have been caught out. *Spoiler alert:* It's not pretty.

## 📖 Why Should You Care About Data Privacy?

You might be wondering, "I'm just starting out. Why should I care about data privacy now?" Well, because whether you're launching a new product, running an app, or managing a side hustle, data privacy impacts everyone.

Here's the deal: regulations like the **GDPR** (General Data Protection Regulation) in Europe or **CCPA** (California Consumer Privacy Act) in the U.S. aren't just for mega-companies. They apply to anyone handling personal data—like emails, browsing history, or purchase behavior. And in today's digital age, **data** is basically currency. So you've got to handle it with care.

If you think, "I'll just deal with this later," let's break down why that's a dangerous game to play.

### *The Big Costs of Non-Compliance: Real-Life Cases*

It's not just about fines (though those can be jaw-dropping). Non-compliance can shut down your operations, hurt your reputation, and make users abandon you faster than they joined. Let's look at some real-life stories of companies that took a data privacy misstep and paid the price—literally.

### 1.     *Google: €50 Million Fine for Lack of Transparency (2019)*

Google—a company we all know—faced one of the first major GDPR penalties. French regulators, led by *CNIL*, imposed a €50 million ($57 million) fine because Google wasn't transparent enough about how they collected, stored, and used people's data. Specifically, they didn't provide enough information in a clear, accessible way about how data was being used to personalize ads. For users, this felt shady because they didn't know exactly what they were agreeing to.

Why is this important for you? Transparency is key. If users feel like they're left in the dark, they're not going to trust your product, no matter how awesome it is.

## 2.     *Meta (Facebook): Record-Breaking €1.2 Billion Fine (2023)*

In 2023, Meta (formerly Facebook) was handed a record-breaking €1.2 billion ($1.3 billion) fine by European regulators. The problem? Meta was transferring data from European users to the U.S. without proper protections in place. This case involved years of back-and-forth with regulators, and it highlighted a key point: data privacy laws aren't just about *what* you collect, but *where* that data goes.

With tech products becoming more global, handling international data properly is a huge deal. If you're aiming to grow your product beyond your home country, you've got to ensure you're respecting the privacy laws of each region.

## 3.     *TikTok: €345 Million Fine for Mishandling Teen Data (2023)*

Gen Z's favorite social app, TikTok, faced a whopping €345 million ($368 million) fine from the EU in 2023. Why? Their settings for teens and kids were too relaxed. TikTok made profiles public by default and didn't offer enough protections for minors. This is a huge deal because younger users are considered more vulnerable, and regulators take that seriously.

This case is especially relevant if your product caters to younger audiences. The lesson? Be extra cautious with how you handle data from minors. Set strict privacy defaults and give users (and their parents) easy control over their settings.

## 4.  *British Airways: £20 Million Fine for Data Breach (2020)*

Now, here's a case from outside the tech industry: British Airways. In 2020, they were fined £20 million ($25 million) by UK regulators for not preventing a data breach that exposed the personal info of over 400,000 customers. It wasn't just that the breach happened (because let's face it, breaches do occur); it's that British Airways didn't act fast enough or have the right security measures in place to prevent it.

So, what's the takeaway here? Even if your product is well-meaning and you're not trying to misuse data, it's crucial to have robust security measures. Data breaches can happen to anyone, and if you don't respond quickly and transparently, you'll be held responsible.

## 5.  *Amazon: Record GDPR Fine of €746 Million (2021)*

Amazon also faced a massive GDPR fine in 2021—this time, €746 million ($865 million). The violation? It was linked to how Amazon used customer data for targeted advertising without proper consent. This fine shows that even tech giants with sophisticated systems can slip up when it comes to compliance.

For you, this example highlights how crucial **user consent** is. If you're planning to use data to target ads, recommend products, or personalize experiences, make sure your users *explicitly* agree to it—and that they can easily opt out if they want to.

### *How Non-Compliance Can Damage Your Brand*

Beyond the massive fines, non-compliance can tarnish your brand image. Customers today care deeply about their privacy, and when they find out a company has mishandled their data, trust goes out the window. In fact, a survey by **Pew Research** found that 79% of U.S. adults are concerned about how their data is being used by companies.

If your customers don't trust you, they're more likely to switch to a competitor that takes data privacy seriously. Think of it this way: would you keep using a product if you found out your personal information wasn't safe?

##  Pro Tips to Stay Compliant

Now that you know what happens when companies drop the ball on data privacy, here's what you can do to avoid these pitfalls:

1. **Get Familiar with Data Privacy Laws**: This might sound boring, but understanding key regulations like GDPR, CCPA, and others is essential. The rules differ depending on where you're operating, so make sure you're up to speed on the laws in your market.

2. **Privacy by Design:** This means building privacy features into your product from the very beginning. Don't wait until launch day to figure this out. Think about how you'll protect user data while designing your app, website, or service.

3. **Be Transparent:** Users should know exactly what data you're collecting, how you're using it, and who you're sharing it with. Make your privacy policy easy to read (no

legal jargon) and make sure it's accessible on your website or app.

4. **Get User Consent:** Always, always get clear consent before collecting or using personal data, especially for things like targeted ads. Bonus points if you make opting in (and out) super simple.

5. **Secure Your Systems:** Prevent data breaches by securing your servers, using encryption, and regularly updating your security protocols. If a breach happens, notify users and authorities right away.

 # What We Learnt

- **AI isn't neutral** – It's only as good as the data it's trained on, and that data often comes with biases. That's why it's super important to create diverse teams and keep monitoring your AI systems to avoid those biases.

- **Bias in AI is real** – Just ask Amazon, who had to ditch an AI tool that favored male candidates for job positions. Oops! The fix? Diverse teams and continuous audits.

- **Transparency builds trust** – No one likes a "black box" AI system. We learned that using explainable AI (XAI) and being clear about how decisions are made makes your users (and regulators) much happier.

- **Accountability matters** – When AI makes a mistake, someone needs to be responsible. We saw how companies like Tesla balance accountability between AI systems and human operators. You should, too.

- **Job displacement is a big deal** – As AI automates more jobs, it's crucial to invest in upskilling and reskilling your workforce to avoid leaving people behind.

- **Accuracy is key** – If your AI isn't accurate, it's more than just a technical fail—it's a trust fail. Continuous testing, real-world validation, and regular updates keep your AI sharp and reliable.

- **Compliance isn't optional** – Global regulations like GDPR and CCPA are serious business. Getting familiar with these rules early on will save you from a world of hurt (and massive fines).

- **Data privacy builds loyalty** – Your users care deeply about how you handle their data. Be transparent, ask for consent, and let them control their own information to build trust and keep your customers happy.

- **Ethical AI is the future** – From reducing bias to ensuring transparency, we've seen how responsible AI is not just a trend—it's the future of product management.

# PART 3:

## AI TOOLS FOR PRODUCT MANAGERS

# CHAPTER 4:
# AI-POWERED MARKET RESEARCH

If you've ever felt like figuring out what your customers want is as tough as trying to crack a secret code, you're not alone! Understanding customer needs used to mean spending endless hours on surveys, interviews, and browsing social media. But now, with AI in the picture, product managers can do it smarter and faster—no crystal ball required.

AI-powered tools are basically like having Sherlock Holmes on your team—except they don't need a trench coat or a magnifying glass. These tools analyze tons of data from social media comments, online reviews, search trends, and even competitor strategies. And instead of just giving you a bunch of numbers, they offer actual insights: "Your audience is talking about sustainable packaging" or "There's growing interest in vegan skincare."

So, let's break down how you can leverage AI not just to stay in the game, but to lead it. Whether it's identifying new trends or spotting untapped markets, AI helps you uncover the "why" behind customer behaviors. And that's not just helpful—it's powerful.

## ⚒ *AI Tools for Market Analysis and Customer Insights*

Picture this: you're working on a new line of eco-friendly sneakers. You need to figure out if customers want bold, vibrant colors or classic, minimalist vibes. In the past, you might have spent hours scrolling through Instagram comments or digging into customer surveys. But now, AI tools can handle this for you, and in real-time.

Tools like **IBM Watson, Sprinklr, and Talkwalker** are like digital detectives on steroids. They don't just scan social media; they dive deep into online reviews, forums, competitor sites, and even niche subreddits, piecing together a comprehensive picture of what customers really think[22]. They reveal the stuff that often gets overlooked: what people love, what they hate, and even the "why-can't-someone-make-this-already?" ideas that could be the next big trend.

But here's where it gets even cooler: these tools don't just track trends; they analyze sentiment. Are customers really feeling the hype about your latest launch, or are they lukewarm? AI tools decode emojis, sarcasm, and context, so you get a nuanced

---

[22] These tools help identify overlooked trends, customer pain points, and new opportunities, enabling proactive adjustments to marketing strategies. For more detailed information, you can explore their official websites: IBM Watson, Sprinklr, and Talkwalker.

understanding of customer emotions—like a personal translator for Gen Z's favorite language: vibes. Want to know what's hot before it hits mainstream? AI can predict trends by analyzing what's buzzing across different channels, from TikTok hashtags to YouTube comments.

It's like having a supercharged data analyst who never sleeps, never gets tired, and doesn't need a venti latte to power through. Whether you're a startup founder, a social media manager, or just someone curious about what's trending, AI tools can be your shortcut to getting real-time customer insights. So, next time you're wondering what the buzz is about, you know exactly where to turn.

## ✖ *AI for Predictive Analytics: Smarter Product Decisions*

Ever wish you could peek into the future to know whether your latest product idea is going to be a hit or a miss? While AI might not help you win the lottery, it *can* help you predict whether your product will fly or flop—well before it even launches. Welcome to the world of predictive analytics, where AI helps you make smarter, more strategic product decisions.

AI tools for predictive analytics don't just look at one or two data points; they dive deep, analyzing everything from historical sales trends and customer behaviors to competitor strategies and even macroeconomic factors. Picture this: you're developing a subscription-based fitness app, and you want to know which features will keep users hooked. AI tools like Tableau, Salesforce Einstein, or Microsoft Azure can sift through mountains of data to identify patterns, offering you insights like, "Hey, 70% of users who don't engage with a feature within the first week are likely to cancel their subscription by month three." This early warning system allows you to make tweaks—like adding more personalized workout plans or better onboarding experiences—before users lose interest.

But it doesn't stop at predicting churn. AI can forecast sales, identify which customer segments are most likely to convert, and even detect which marketing strategies are likely to resonate with your audience. Say you're debating whether to launch a new feature or double down on an existing one. Predictive analytics can weigh the options based on past data, ongoing trends, and customer feedback, giving you a clear view of which path has the best odds of success.

For founders and product managers, this means no more guessing games. Want to know if a trend—like eco-friendly packaging or gamified experiences—is just a fad or a long-term shift? AI's got you covered. It looks at evolving trends across social media, e-commerce platforms, and user reviews, helping you adapt your strategy before trends go mainstream.

AI also makes the numbers less scary. By transforming complex data into visual dashboards, it's like having a cheat sheet that simplifies everything. It can show you not just *what* might happen, but also *why*—like pinpointing that users are dropping off because the checkout process is too long or a key feature isn't working as expected. With AI, you're not just reacting to problems after they happen; you're anticipating them and making preemptive moves.

So, whether you're fine-tuning your app's features or planning your next product launch, AI-powered predictive analytics helps you stay ahead of the curve. It's like having a GPS for product success: guiding you with insights, showing you the best route, and warning you about potential roadblocks before you even get there.

# 🔍 Real-Life Example: Unilever's AI Approach

Let's break it down with a real-world example: Unilever, a global giant in consumer goods, is using AI to stay one step ahead of the competition. With a brand lineup that includes household names like Dove, Axe, and Ben & Jerry's, Unilever isn't just relying on old-school methods to understand what customers want—they're going all-in with AI to spot trends and adapt fast.

***Here's how it works***: Unilever uses AI tools like Signal AI to analyze social media conversations, customer reviews, and even global news trends. These AI tools don't just collect data—they *decipher* it, turning countless customer comments and reviews into actionable insights. For example, if AI picks up a surge in conversations around "sustainable packaging," Unilever can shift gears quickly. They might fast-track the development of eco-friendly packaging options or even launch new product lines focused on sustainability. This approach keeps Unilever ahead of the curve, ensuring they're not just reacting to trends but actually leading them.

The cool part? AI doesn't just tell Unilever *what* people are talking about; it reveals *how* they're talking about it. Is the sentiment around sustainable packaging overwhelmingly positive, or are customers frustrated by the lack of options? AI can break down the tone, emotion, and even the context of conversations, providing a deeper understanding of consumer feelings. This level of insight helps Unilever tailor marketing campaigns, tweak product features, and even decide which regions to target based on emerging demands.

For product managers, this is a game-changer. Imagine having AI tools that give you a sneak peek into what's trending right now—and what's likely to be hot next year. It's like having a radar that alerts you to shifting consumer desires before competitors even know what's happening. Want to know if the hype around plant-based ingredients is just a trend or a long-term demand? AI tools can analyze social media buzz, industry reports, and even customer feedback to give you a clear answer.

The broader lesson? AI-powered insights aren't just about keeping up with the market; they're about shaping it. By identifying shifts in customer sentiment and trends early, you can make smarter product decisions, create marketing campaigns that resonate, and introduce features that your audience didn't even know they wanted. It's like having a crystal ball for product strategy—except this one is backed by data, not guesswork. So, whether you're managing a small startup or a billion-dollar brand, AI can be your strategic sidekick, helping you stay relevant, adaptable, and ahead of the game.

# Conclusion:

As a product manager, embracing AI tools isn't just about keeping up; it's about leading the charge. AI doesn't replace your creativity or intuition—it simply turbocharges it. So, the next time you're digging for customer insights or tweaking your product strategy, think of AI as your sidekick that's got your back, ready to help you make smarter, faster decisions.

 **What We Learnt**

- **AI simplifies market research**: AI tools offer a faster and smarter way to understand customer needs by analyzing vast data sources like social media, online reviews, and search trends.

- **AI provides deeper insights**: Instead of just raw data, AI tools present actionable insights—like emerging trends, customer sentiment, and even new product ideas.

- **Real-time customer analysis**: AI tools can analyze customer preferences in real time, breaking down sentiment, context, and even emojis to decode consumer "vibes."

- **Predictive analytics for better decisions**: AI's predictive analytics help forecast customer behavior, potential sales, and successful product features, minimizing risks in product launches.

- **Strategic foresight**: AI identifies whether trends are fleeting fads or long-term shifts, enabling proactive, data-driven strategies for product management.

- **AI-powered case study**: Real-world example of Unilever shows how AI tools help companies analyze trends, understand customer sentiment, and make informed product adjustments quickly.

- **Enhanced product management**: AI tools offer product managers a data-backed advantage, transforming guesswork into clear, actionable strategies.

- **AI boosts efficiency, not creativity**: While AI speeds up decision-making and analysis, it complements rather than replaces the creativity and intuition of product managers.

# CHAPTER 5:
# AI-DRIVEN PRODUCT STRATEGIES

In today's world, technology doesn't just support our lives—it *drives* them. From the apps you scroll through in the morning to the algorithms that power your personalized playlists, AI has become the secret ingredient behind almost every product you use. So, when it comes to building your own product strategies, aligning with AI isn't just an advantage anymore—it's a *necessity*.

You've seen how AI has redefined industries, transformed user experiences, and boosted growth across sectors. Companies like Amazon use AI to optimize logistics, while Instagram uses it to deliver personalized content. The goal? Making things smarter, faster, and tailored to your customers' needs. But now, it's your turn.

How can you use AI to create smarter products, better user journeys, and more impactful strategies? This chapter will break it all down for you in a relatable, step-by-step way.

First, let's talk about the *why* behind AI-powered strategies. AI isn't just about fancy algorithms or complicated models—it's about creating real value for users. Think of AI as a supercharged decision-making tool, one that helps you not only solve today's problems but also anticipate tomorrow's needs. It's about thinking ahead, understanding trends before they peak, and making data-backed decisions that hit the mark.

Imagine you're working on a new product launch. Instead of relying solely on traditional market research, AI tools can help you analyze customer sentiment, predict demand shifts, and even tailor marketing messages based on user behavior patterns. AI helps you get closer to your users, understanding not just *what* they want, but *why* they want it, and even predicting what they'll want next.

In this chapter, we'll dive into specific AI tools and methodologies that can shape your product strategies. Whether it's using machine learning to analyze user data for insights, implementing natural language processing (NLP) to understand customer feedback more accurately, or deploying predictive analytics to foresee market trends, we'll cover it all. Plus, we'll share some practical tips on how to use AI responsibly, ensuring that your strategies not only resonate with users but also align with ethical AI principles.

Let's not forget about collaboration—AI isn't just for data scientists or engineers. It's a tool that product managers, marketers, designers, and stakeholders can all benefit from. We'll explore how cross-functional teams can leverage AI together to create truly innovative products. In this new era, the most successful product managers are the ones who know how to translate AI's potential into strategies that feel intuitive, human, and deeply connected to user needs.

So, get ready to level up your strategy game. By the end of this chapter, you'll not only understand AI's role in product management but also feel confident in using it to create data-driven, forward-thinking products that genuinely stand out in the market. Ready to dive in? Let's go!

## 🛠 *Crafting AI-Centric Product Visions and Roadmaps*

Imagine plotting your product's trajectory over the next five years. In the past, you might have relied on gut feelings, user feedback, and a splash of competitive analysis to guide the way. But today, AI has shifted the playing field, giving you powerful tools like predictive analytics, natural language processing (NLP), and machine learning models that can forecast market demands and anticipate user behavior shifts more accurately than ever before. Let's break down how you can fully leverage AI to create a more robust, insightful, and agile product roadmap.

### *Setting the AI Vision*

Start with a simple question: what problems can AI solve that traditional methods can't? AI has the unique ability to automate repetitive tasks, analyze large data sets, offer hyper-personalization, and improve decision-making processes. Think about companies like Amazon, which uses AI to predict the products you're likely to buy next, or Grammarly, which leverages AI to help users improve their writing in real time. Similarly, you could use AI to identify patterns in user behavior, automate customer service with chatbots, or even detect anomalies in financial transactions if you're in the fintech space.

At this stage, your product vision should be clear about not just what you aim to achieve but also how AI will enable you to reach these goals faster and more effectively. For instance, imagine you're building a health app—AI could help analyze user symptoms, suggest potential diagnoses, and even connect users to specialists. This doesn't just improve the user experience; it transforms it.

## Building AI-Enhanced Roadmaps

Once you've set your AI-centric vision, it's time to translate it into a dynamic roadmap. AI tools can help you prioritize features and identify gaps by analyzing historical data, user interactions, and evolving market trends. For example, take Duolingo, which uses machine learning to tailor lessons based on your progress and struggles. Similarly, if you're developing a learning app, AI can recommend personalized content based on user performance and engagement, making the learning process more adaptive and engaging.

Unlike traditional roadmaps that are often rigid and linear, AI-enhanced roadmaps are more flexible and responsive. Imagine you're working on a ride-hailing app. By using AI to analyze user demand, weather patterns, and traffic data, you can adjust your roadmap to launch features like predictive ride estimates or heat maps for ride demand. The key here is to be ready to pivot based on AI-generated insights, making your roadmap less of a strict itinerary and more of a living, breathing document that adapts as you go.

## Fueling Product Innovation with AI

With AI, real-time data becomes a game-changer. Think about how Waze uses AI to provide real-time traffic updates, rerouting drivers based on current conditions. Similarly, for a fitness app, AI could analyze user activity data to suggest optimal workout times or identify when users are most likely to skip a workout, offering motivational nudges. By tapping into real-time data, your product stays relevant and responsive to the ever-changing needs of users.

🔍 **For example**, you are using a budgeting app called *PennyWise*, where AI tracks your spending in real time. Midway through the month, AI notices you've already spent $450 of your $500 dining budget. It promptly sends a notification: "You're close to your dining budget for the month. Consider eating in to avoid overspending." Later, a sudden $200 charge at an unfamiliar restaurant pops up, prompting AI to alert you: "This transaction seems unusual. Was it you?" If you confirm it wasn't, it suggests checking for potential fraud. By continuously monitoring and adapting, *PennyWise* keeps your finances on track, offering timely, practical insights tailored to your habits.

## ✖ *Using AI for Insights*

Market research is a critical part of shaping your product strategy. However, it can be prone to errors or blind spots, especially when relying on manual methods. AI is changing that by shifting your approach from reactive to proactive, offering sharper insights and more accurate predictions.

### *Leveraging AI for Real-Time Insights*

AI tools can process massive datasets in real-time, uncovering trends and consumer needs more rapidly than traditional methods. For instance, consider a small food startup analyzing customer feedback on Yelp or Google Reviews. Instead of manually sifting through hundreds of reviews, the startup can use Natural Language Processing (NLP) tools to instantly detect trends like growing interest in vegan options or common complaints about delivery times. This immediate analysis enables the company to tweak its menu, refine its delivery process, or introduce new dishes based on popular demand—right when it matters.

## Segmentation and Personalization at Scale

One of AI's standout features in market research is its ability to segment audiences based on behavior, preferences, and demographics. Let's say you're working in the healthcare sector, developing a new fitness app aimed at improving heart health. AI-powered clustering algorithms can identify distinct user segments, such as seniors focusing on low-impact exercises, millennials interested in high-intensity interval training (HIIT), or parents looking for family-friendly workouts. This kind of precise segmentation allows you to create tailored campaigns and product features that truly resonate with each group.

## Predictive Analytics for Strategic Forecasting

AI's strength isn't limited to analyzing past data—it can also predict future market movements. Imagine an e-commerce business specializing in seasonal fashion. Using AI tools like time-series analysis, the business can forecast demand for winter coats based on historical sales, weather patterns, and social media trends. As a result, the company can stock up on inventory and launch marketing campaigns ahead of the winter season, staying prepared for increased demand instead of scrambling at the last minute.

🔍 **For example**, imagine *Brew Bliss*[23], a local coffee shop known for its cozy atmosphere but eager to attract more

---

[23] AI-driven tools allow businesses like Brew Bliss to analyze extensive customer feedback from various platforms such as Yelp, Google, and social media. For more

customers beyond its loyal regulars. To do this, they turn to AI-driven market research. Instead of manually reading through thousands of online reviews, *Brew Bliss* uses an AI tool that scans customer feedback on Yelp, Google, and even social media. The AI swiftly identifies key trends, like a rising demand for plant-based milk alternatives, such as oat and almond milk, and consistent complaints about long wait times during the morning rush.

With these insights, *Brew Bliss* can immediately adapt— introducing more plant-based milk options to cater to dietary preferences while also rethinking its morning workflow to serve customers faster. Additionally, AI helps segment their audience more accurately, identifying distinct customer groups like on-the-go professionals, college students craving affordable caffeine, and retirees enjoying leisurely mornings. Using this information, *Brew Bliss* tailors its marketing campaigns, offering coffee subscriptions for busy workers, finals week discounts for students, and relaxed "Morning Chat" sessions for retirees.

Finally, predictive analytics help *Brew Bliss* prepare for the future. The AI analyzes weather patterns, past sales, and local events, forecasting a colder-than-usual winter. With this knowledge, *Brew Bliss* stocks up on hot beverage ingredients, launches a "Stay Cozy" promotion, and adjusts staffing schedules to meet the anticipated demand spike. Thanks to AI, *Brew Bliss* evolves from a reactive business into a proactive, customer-centric brand, continuously

---

information about AI-driven tools analyzing customer feedback, you can visit SurveyMonkey Genius

adapting to changing market trends and staying ahead of competitors.

## 🛠 *Predicting Future Trends and User Behaviors with AI Insights*

Anticipating user needs before they're even aware of them is the ultimate goal for any product manager. In today's fast-paced, digital-first world, AI offers a significant advantage. With its advanced predictive capabilities, AI can provide insights into evolving user behavior, helping you stay ahead of the curve. Imagine having a tool that not only analyzes user interactions but also predicts the next steps they're likely to take, making your products smarter, faster, and more user-centric.

### *Using AI to Model User Journeys*

AI can process vast amounts of past user data to identify patterns and predict future interactions. This means you can create smoother, more personalized user journeys that drive higher engagement, retention, and satisfaction. For example, AI can detect when users typically drop off in a sign-up flow and suggest improvements, such as simplifying forms or adjusting the placement of CTAs (calls to action) to boost conversion rates.

### *Trend Analysis and Forecasting*

Unlike traditional methods that depend mainly on past data, AI taps into a blend of historical data and real-time signals to predict future trends. This allows you to not only react to emerging trends but also proactively shape your product strategy. Imagine you're managing an app, and AI detects a sudden uptick in searches related to a new social media feature. With this insight, you can consider developing similar functionalities within your app to align with shifting user preferences. This kind of forecasting can help you keep up with evolving demands, whether it's the rise of voice-based interfaces, prioritization of eco-friendly features, or shifts toward AR/VR experiences.

## *Behavioral Insights from AI*

Deep learning models excel at analyzing user behavior in granular detail, identifying key triggers that influence actions like conversion, engagement, or even churn. AI can help you identify which features are most valuable to users, prompting you to refine or expand them. For instance, if AI analytics show that users frequently engage with a specific feature during a trial period, you might make that feature more prominent in the onboarding flow, ultimately increasing user satisfaction and retention.

> 🔍 *For example*, consider Spotify's use of AI for personalized music recommendations. By analyzing individual listening habits, as well as broader trends across its user base, Spotify uses AI to create curated playlists like "Discover Weekly" or "Daily Mix." These playlists often introduce users to new tracks or artists they might enjoy, keeping engagement high and increasing the likelihood of users subscribing to premium plans. By offering this deeply personalized experience, Spotify maintains a strong connection with its users, ensuring they feel understood and catered to at every interaction. This approach demonstrates how AI can be a game-changer, enabling you to deliver a tailored experience that meets user needs, even as they evolve.

## ⚙ Practical Steps for Implementing AI-Driven Strategies

### *Invest in the Right AI Tools*

Before implementing AI strategies, ensure you have the right tools. Whether it's using machine learning for predictive analytics, NLP for sentiment analysis, or AI-powered CRMs, select tools that align with your product goals.

### *Train Your Teams*

AI isn't just about tools—it's about people. Ensure your product teams understand AI's potential and limitations. Invest in training sessions that help your team effectively use AI tools, interpret AI-generated insights, and adapt strategies based on data.

### *Measure and Iterate*

AI-driven strategies require continuous monitoring and iteration. Establish clear metrics to track the effectiveness of your AI tools and methodologies. Use these insights to refine your strategies over time, ensuring they remain relevant and impactful.

# What We Learnt

- **AI is Your New Best Friend for Strategy:** AI isn't just tech—it's a game-changer. It helps you build smarter, faster, and more personalized products that truly connect with users.

- **Predicting What Users Want:** AI gives you superpowers to understand user behavior and trends. It helps you anticipate what users need even before they know it themselves!

- **Creating Dynamic Product Roadmaps:** AI tools like predictive analytics and NLP make your product roadmap more flexible and responsive, letting you pivot based on real-time insights.

- **Real-World AI Wins:** From predicting demand to segmenting users, AI is there to guide you every step of the way, making your product strategy more relevant and engaging.

- **AI is a Team Effort:** It's not just for data scientists—AI is for everyone. Whether you're a product manager, designer, or marketer, AI helps all team members collaborate better.

- **Practical Steps to Get Started:** Choose the right AI tools, train your team, and continuously refine your approach to make sure your strategies stay ahead of the curve.

# CHAPTER 6:
## ENHANCING USER EXPERIENCE WITH AI

Artificial Intelligence (AI) is the game-changer in user experience (UX) design today. Whether you're a newbie Product Manager (PM) or a pro, leveraging AI can transform your product's UX from average to exceptional. In this chapter, we'll break down how AI not only helps you optimize user interactions but also ensures a more personalized experience that keeps users coming back for more.

# 📖 Why AI Matters for UX Design

Imagine having a superpower that allows you to anticipate what your users need before they even realize it themselves. That's essentially what AI offers in the world of UX. AI goes beyond traditional data analysis by identifying patterns in user behavior, predicting user needs, and offering personalized solutions. With AI, you can create products that not only meet users' expectations but often exceed them.

Think of AI as your behind-the-scenes teammate. It works around the clock, analyzing vast amounts of user data to offer insights you'd never discover manually. This makes it an essential part of any PM's toolkit. Here are some core benefits AI brings to UX design:

- **Personalization**: Tailors content and features based on individual user behavior.

- **Efficiency**: Speeds up the product development process by automating repetitive tasks.

- **Predictive Insights**: Helps you understand and anticipate user needs.

- **Improved Interaction**: Makes the product more interactive and responsive, often using chatbots or virtual assistants.

# 📖 The Basics of AI in UX

Before we dive into real-life applications, let's quickly clarify what we mean by AI in UX.

In simple terms, AI in UX refers to algorithms and machine learning models that analyze user data to create meaningful, context-driven experiences. It could be anything from predictive search results, to chatbots handling customer service inquiries, or even voice assistants offering recommendations based on user history.

For example, AI can detect when users are struggling with a feature. It can then prompt helpful tips or redirect them to another part of the app where they're more likely to engage. AI basically creates a feedback loop that keeps learning from user behavior to improve the product in real-time.

## 📖 *Real-World Example: How Facebook Uses AI to Optimize UX*

Let's take a closer look at how Facebook uses AI to enhance its UX. It's no secret that Facebook's News Feed is powered by AI, but the depth of its application is remarkable. Every interaction—likes, comments, shares, and even the time you spend on a post—is fed into a machine learning algorithm that's designed to optimize the feed in real-time.

Here's how it works:

- **Data Collection**: Every click, scroll, or interaction on Facebook is collected as data. AI algorithms then process this data to identify patterns of user interest.

- **Content Personalization**: Based on these patterns, Facebook decides what to show users in their News Feed. If you spend more time engaging with travel content, you'll see more of it.

- **Feature Optimization**: Facebook uses AI insights to improve its features. For instance, if users frequently react to a specific type of post, the platform can tweak the algorithm to show similar content more often, boosting engagement.

The key takeaway for PMs is that AI enables Facebook to deliver a highly personalized experience that aligns with user preferences—improving overall engagement and satisfaction.

# 📖 AI-Powered UX Strategies for PMs

## *1.    Behavioral Analysis for Personalization*

One of the most powerful ways AI enhances UX is through behavioral analysis. This involves tracking user actions—clicks, navigation paths, and even the time spent on different pages—to understand their interests and preferences. As a PM, you can use this data to design personalized user journeys.

**How to Implement:**

- **AI Tools**: Use AI-powered analytics tools like Mixpanel or Amplitude. These tools can identify patterns in user behavior and suggest changes in UX design to better cater to individual users.

- **Real-World Use**: Think about how Spotify recommends music based on your listening habits. AI models analyze everything from your most-played tracks to how long you listen before skipping to another song. You can apply similar logic to your product by tailoring recommendations based on user interactions.

## 2. *Chatbots & Virtual Assistants for Real-Time Support*

Gone are the days when users waited hours for customer support. AI-powered chatbots and virtual assistants provide instant, 24/7 support, making users feel heard and valued.

**How to Implement:**

- **Conversational AI:** Integrate AI chatbots like Drift or Intercom into your product. These chatbots can handle frequently asked questions, guide users through the app, and even offer product demos.

- **Real-World Use:** Consider how Netflix uses chatbots to handle customer support inquiries about subscription issues, playback errors, or billing. By using conversational AI, Netflix reduces response time and boosts user satisfaction, which you can replicate in your product's support system.

## 3. *Predictive Analytics for Anticipating User Needs*

Imagine being able to predict what users want before they even ask for it. AI's predictive analytics make this possible by analyzing user data and forecasting future behavior.

**How to Implement:**

- **User Cohorts**: Use predictive models to create user cohorts—groups of users with similar behaviors or interests. Tailor features or marketing campaigns to these specific cohorts to increase engagement.

- **Real-World Use**: Amazon uses predictive analytics to recommend products you might be interested in, based on your past purchases and browsing history. This enhances UX by making the shopping experience seamless and intuitive.

# 4. *Voice & Gesture Recognition for More Natural Interaction*

AI can enable more natural user interactions through voice or gesture recognition, making UX more accessible and user-friendly. This is especially useful for products aimed at diverse audiences, including older users or people with disabilities.

**How to Implement:**

- **Voice UX Design**: Integrate voice recognition technologies like Google Assistant or Amazon Alexa. For apps targeting users who prefer hands-free interaction, this can be a huge plus.

- **Gesture Controls**: Use AI algorithms to detect gestures (like swiping or tapping) for navigation. This can be particularly useful in mobile apps, where user interaction is primarily gesture-based.

# 5. *A/B Testing with AI for Better UX Optimization*

A/B testing has always been a part of the PM's toolkit, but AI takes it to the next level by continuously learning from user interactions and making real-time adjustments.

**How to Implement:**

- **Automated Testing**: Use AI-powered tools like Optimizely or VWO that allow you to run A/B tests automatically. These tools can test different UI elements, button placements, or calls-to-action, and then suggest which version performs best.

- **Real-World Use**: Think of how Airbnb uses AI for A/B testing different layouts, colors, and navigation flows. It helps Airbnb identify the best version of its app interface, resulting in higher booking rates and better user satisfaction.

## 6.  *Ethical Considerations: AI and User Privacy*

While AI can significantly enhance UX, it's crucial to use it ethically. AI relies heavily on user data, which means PMs need to be mindful of data privacy laws and ethical AI practices.

**Key Points to Remember:**

- **Transparency**: Clearly inform users about how their data will be used. Avoid overly complex jargon and keep it straightforward.

- **Consent**: Always obtain user consent before collecting data, whether for personalized recommendations or other AI-driven features.

- **Bias Mitigation**: AI models can reflect biases present in the data. Make sure your AI models are regularly audited and trained on diverse datasets to avoid perpetuating biases.

## 7.  *Actionable Takeaways for PMs*

- **Start Small**: If you're new to AI, start with simple integrations like AI-driven analytics tools or basic chatbots.

- **Stay User-Centric**: Always keep the user at the center of your AI strategies. AI is just a tool to enhance UX; it's not the UX itself.

- **Iterate Constantly**: AI thrives on continuous learning. Regularly update your AI models to align with changing user behavior and feedback.

- **Ethical AI**: Make AI decisions with user privacy in mind, and be transparent about data usage.

## *Conclusion: AI as Your Co-Pilot for UX*

Incorporating AI into your product's UX isn't just about making things more efficient; it's about delivering a genuinely valuable experience to your users. By embracing AI, you can create products that are not only functional but also intuitive, personalized, and responsive. As you dive into AI-enhanced UX, remember that the goal is to make users feel understood and appreciated, ensuring they keep coming back for more.

**What We Learnt**

- **AI is Your UX Ally:** It's the behind-the-scenes magic that helps you deliver personalized, efficient, and user-friendly experiences.

- **Super-Powered Personalization:** AI tailors content based on user behavior, making the product feel like it was made *just* for the user.

- **Better & Faster Decisions:** AI analyzes tons of user data 24/7, giving you insights that help you design better UX, faster.

- **Real-Time Support, Anytime:** AI chatbots and virtual assistants offer 24/7 support, making users feel valued and improving engagement.

- **Predict the Future:** AI's predictive analytics allow you to anticipate user needs, so you can deliver solutions before users even ask for them.

- **Natural Interactions:** AI-driven voice and gesture recognition create more intuitive, accessible user interactions.

- **Smarter A/B Testing:** AI makes A/B testing more effective by learning from user behavior and suggesting real-time tweaks.

- **Ethical AI Usage:** Always prioritize user privacy, get clear consent, and work to minimize bias in AI models.

- **Start Small & Scale Up:** If you're new to AI, start with simple tools and features—like chatbots or AI analytics—before diving deeper.

- **Iterate & Improve:** AI keeps learning, so your UX should too! Regularly update your models based on user behavior and feedback.

- **AI Isn't the UX; It's the Tool:** Always keep users at the center of your strategy, using AI to make the experience better—not replace it.

# CHAPTER 7:
# COLLABORATING WITH AI TEAMS

## 📖 Bridging the Gap Between Business and AI/Tech Teams

So, you're stepping into the exciting world of AI product management! As you navigate this terrain, you'll often find yourself at the intersection of business goals and technical expertise. Your job? Bridging the gap. But how exactly do you do that without feeling lost in translation?

**Understand the Language:** Start by getting comfortable with the basics of AI terminology. It's not about becoming a data scientist yourself, but rather understanding enough to hold your own in conversations. Terms like "machine learning models," "training data," and "neural networks" will often pop up in meetings. While it might seem like a different dialect at first, having a foundational understanding helps you communicate your vision better.

📌 ***Pro Tip:*** Spend some time on platforms like Coursera or Udemy, which offer short courses on AI fundamentals. Even a crash course can make a difference!

**Embrace the Mindset:** AI teams often approach problems differently than business or marketing teams. While business teams think about customer pain points and ROI, AI teams are more focused on the accuracy, precision, and feasibility of models. The key to bridging this gap is empathy. Understand their challenges—like dealing with biased data or training an underperforming model. When you acknowledge these issues, it fosters better communication and trust.

**Build Relationships:** Like any successful collaboration, it all starts with solid relationships. Set up informal chats, maybe even over a coffee or virtual hangout, to get to know your AI counterparts. This casual rapport can often help break down communication barriers and make collaboration smoother.

## ⚙️ Best Practices for Effective Collaboration

Collaborating effectively with data scientists and engineers isn't just about aligning on goals; it's about creating a workflow that's mutually beneficial. Here are some proven ways to make it work:

## 1. *Be Clear About Business Objectives*

You need to make sure that the AI team understands the 'why' behind a product or feature. Why is it essential for users? Why does it matter to the business? Once the technical team gets this bigger picture, they can tailor their models and outputs to better suit customer needs.

Let's say you're working on a personalized recommendation feature for an e-commerce platform. Explain to your AI team how personalized recommendations can lead to higher sales, increase customer satisfaction, and reduce churn. By tying the technical objectives back to clear business outcomes, you create a sense of purpose for everyone involved.

## 2. *Adopt an Iterative Approach*

AI is a constantly evolving field. That's why it's best to embrace an iterative approach, where you continuously refine models based on new data and insights. Rather than expecting a perfect model right from the start, encourage a "test and learn" culture.

> 🔍 ***Real-World Insight***: Companies like Spotify have successfully adopted iterative collaboration between product managers and AI teams. PMs provide insights based on user feedback, and data scientists tweak algorithms to enhance the listening experience based on the feedback. This keeps the process dynamic and responsive.

## 3. *Stay User-Centric*

While it's easy to get lost in the technical side of things, always bring the focus back to the end-user. Ask questions like:

- How does this model improve user experience?
- Is it making the product more accessible?
- Are there any biases in the model that could affect specific user groups?

📌 *Pro Tip:* Encourage the AI team to join user testing sessions whenever possible. Seeing real users interact with the AI-powered features often inspires new ideas and improvements.

## 4.   *Align on Metrics and KPIs*

Effective collaboration means aligning on success metrics. While data scientists might focus on metrics like accuracy, precision, and recall, you as the product manager should ensure that these technical metrics align with business metrics like user engagement, revenue growth, or conversion rates.

🔍 *For example*, if you're building a fraud detection system, the AI team might emphasize false positives/negatives, while you're more focused on reducing fraud-related losses. Aligning these metrics ensures that the AI solutions contribute directly to business goals.

## 5.   *Enable Access to Clean Data*

Data is the fuel that powers AI models. Without access to clean, relevant, and updated data, even the best models will struggle to perform well. As a product manager, it's your role to facilitate access to quality data for the AI team.

This might mean working with data engineers to set up data pipelines or collaborating with legal teams to ensure compliance with data privacy regulations. Having clean, well-annotated data not only speeds up the development process but also leads to better model performance.

🔍 *Example:* At Netflix, product managers work closely with data engineers to ensure that recommendation models have access to the right data at the right time. This collaboration helps personalize user recommendations and enhance the overall viewing experience.

## 6.    *Regular Sync-Ups and Feedback Loops*

Set up regular sync meetings to ensure everyone is on the same page. These can be weekly check-ins, sprint reviews, or more informal feedback sessions. The goal is to keep communication lines open and make adjustments as needed.

Encourage two-way feedback. Let the AI team share technical constraints, while you provide insights on business needs or user feedback. This exchange not only improves the AI model but also helps maintain alignment.

🔍 *Example:* In Microsoft's Azure AI projects, product managers hold bi-weekly check-ins with data scientists and engineers to review model performance, user feedback, and upcoming priorities. This keeps everyone aligned and helps avoid last-minute surprises[24].

---

[24] Microsoft Azure AI projects hold bi-weekly check-ins among product managers, data scientists, and engineers to review model performance and align priorities. This regular collaboration helps maintain model quality and avoid surprises
TECHCOMMUNITY.MICROSOFT.COM Azure

## 7.    *Encourage Experimentation and Innovation*

AI thrives on experimentation. Encourage your AI team to explore new techniques or algorithms that could improve your product. You can support this by creating a safe environment where it's okay to fail fast and learn from it.

Google's product managers, for instance, work closely with AI teams by providing them with resources for rapid prototyping and testing. This experimentation culture allows for innovative solutions that wouldn't have been possible in a more rigid structure.

## 8.    *Celebrate Wins Together*

It's essential to acknowledge and celebrate the achievements of the AI team. Did the new algorithm improve conversion rates by 10%? Awesome! Make sure to highlight it in team meetings, share the news with stakeholders, and give credit where it's due.

> *Culture Hack:* Some companies, like Salesforce, host "AI demo days" where data scientists showcase their work, and PMs get a chance to see the progress up close. It's a fun way to build team morale and foster a collaborative environment.

# 📌  Case Study: Microsoft Azure and AI-Driven Tools

Microsoft's Azure cloud services serve as an excellent example of effective collaboration between product managers and AI teams. Azure uses AI-driven tools to enhance performance and offer better services to its customers. Here's how it works:

1. **Setting the Vision:** Product managers define the overarching goals, such as improving the accuracy of Azure's predictive analytics features.

2. **Engaging AI Teams:** AI teams, including data scientists and ML engineers, collaborate closely with PMs to understand customer pain points, ensuring AI solutions are aligned with business needs.

3. **Iterative Model Development:** Azure AI models are continuously trained and refined based on new customer data and feedback. This iterative approach allows product managers to deliver better performance and user experience with each update.

4. **Shared Metrics:** Both AI and product teams align on metrics, such as reducing latency in AI-driven processes or improving accuracy in predictive analytics, ensuring that the technical and business goals are in sync.

This approach has enabled Microsoft to build AI solutions that are not only powerful but also incredibly user-centric.


## *Final Thoughts: Mastering AI Collaboration*

Collaborating with AI teams is more than just technical coordination; it's about fostering a culture of mutual respect, shared goals, and continuous learning. As a product manager, you're the bridge between the tech world and the business side. By adopting best practices, staying user-centric, and keeping communication lines open, you can create AI-powered products that deliver real value to users.

*Remember:* The future of AI product management isn't just about algorithms—it's about people working together to create smarter, more intuitive solutions. So, be curious, stay adaptable, and never stop learning!

##  What We Learnt

- **Speak AI's Language:** You don't need to be an AI expert, but understanding basic AI terms will help you communicate your ideas better.

- **Build Solid Relationships:** Get to know your AI teammates; it makes communication smoother and collaboration easier.

- **Align Goals:** Make sure both business objectives and AI metrics are clear and aligned from the start.

- **Iterative Wins:** AI thrives on testing and refining, so embrace a "learn as you go" mindset.

- **Focus on Users:** Always bring discussions back to the end-user—AI solutions should solve real user problems, not just technical ones.

- **Ensure Clean Data:** Better data equals better AI. Work with data engineers to provide clean, reliable, and relevant data for models.

- **Frequent Sync-Ups:** Regular check-ins with AI teams keep everyone aligned and reduce last-minute surprises.

- **Celebrate Together:** When AI improvements lead to business wins, make sure to highlight them and share the credit.

- **Encourage Innovation:** Give your AI team room to experiment, even if it means failing fast. It often leads to the best solutions!

- **Stay Adaptable:** AI evolves fast, so keep learning and adapting your strategies to stay ahead.

# CHAPTER 8:
## STREAMLINING PRODUCT DEVELOPMENT WITH AI

In the world of product development, one rule dominates: **move fast, fail fast, and improve even faster**. It's not just about building a product; it's about doing it with speed, precision, and innovation. This is where **Artificial Intelligence (AI)** comes into play. AI is no longer an experimental luxury; it's now the workhorse for companies like Google, Amazon, and Slack, helping them streamline their product development processes.

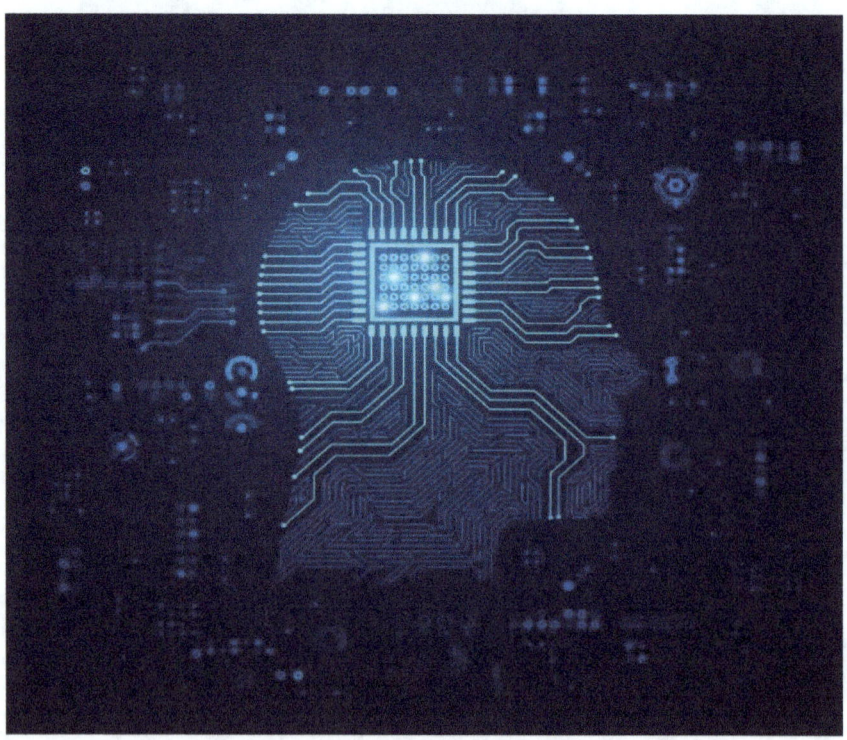

In this chapter, we'll unpack how AI can enhance each phase of product development, from ideation to launch, with real-world tools, examples, and tips. By the end, you'll not only walk away with new knowledge but also fresh ideas to implement in your own product journeys!

## 📖 Why AI Matters in Product Development

So why should you care about AI? The simple answer: **AI speeds things up, reduces errors, and helps you make smarter decisions.** But let's break that down a bit more:

- **AI automates repetitive tasks**: AI handles those boring, time-consuming jobs like data crunching and status updates, freeing you up for strategic thinking and creative problem-solving.

- **AI enhances decision-making**: It helps you analyze massive amounts of data in real-time, finding patterns that might take you weeks to spot. AI gives you insights faster, which means quicker iterations and better products.

- **AI encourages innovation**: By providing predictions, analyzing user feedback, and identifying trends, AI sparks new ideas and concepts that might not come up in a regular brainstorming session.

Now that you know why AI is important, let's dive into how you can actually use it at different stages of product development.

### 1. Ideation: Using AI to Supercharge Creativity

AI in ideation might sound like a contradiction—after all, isn't creativity a human trait? But AI can be a powerful tool for expanding your creative horizons.

## *How AI Works in Ideation:*

- **AI Content Generators:** Tools like **ChatGPT, Jasper, and Writesonic** are excellent brainstorming buddies. By feeding in prompts like user needs, market trends, and potential pain points, these tools generate fresh ideas for product features, messaging, or user experiences.

- **Pattern Recognition with AI:** AI tools like **Crimson Hexagon** scan social media conversations, online forums, and user reviews to find trending topics, unmet needs, or emerging desires. This means you can identify gaps in the market before your competitors do.

- **Customer Feedback Analysis:** AI can analyze reviews, feedback forms, and surveys, organizing insights into themes that point toward potential product features or improvements.

🔍 **Example in Action:** Google's product teams use AI models to scan user feedback from various channels, finding trends and unmet needs. For instance, AI algorithms can analyze millions of reviews and detect patterns, like frequent mentions of a missing feature or a common problem users face. This gives Google a massive edge in ideation, as they know what users want before even starting development.

📌 *Pro Tip*: While AI can suggest ideas, make sure to filter them through human creativity. AI might come up with ideas that are a bit too "out there," so it's essential to evaluate them for feasibility and user appeal.

## 2. *Research: Deep Diving into Market Insights with AI*

Research is the foundation of any product. The better your research, the stronger your product will be. And this is where AI can shine brightest.

### *AI Tools for Research:*

- **AI Sentiment Analysis Tools:** Tools like **Talkwalker and Sprinklr** can analyze customer sentiment across social media, review sites, and forums. This provides a snapshot of what your target audience feels about a specific product, feature, or even your competitors.

- **AI in Competitive Analysis:** AI scrapers can help analyze your competitors' websites, social media, and even their codebases (for open-source projects). AI tools like **SimilarWeb** can provide data on competitor traffic, engagement, and popular content.

- **AI Survey Analysis:** Tools like **SurveyMonkey Genius** analyze survey results quickly, summarizing user opinions and suggesting correlations that would be difficult for a human researcher to detect.

🔍 **Example in Action:** Amazon uses AI to sift through user reviews, browsing histories, and purchasing behaviors to determine what products users love, what they hate, and what's missing in the market. This has led to the development of new features in Alexa or even entirely new Amazon Basics products based on user needs.

📌 ***Pro Tip:*** AI can provide a lot of data, but it's up to you to decide what's relevant. It's easy to get overwhelmed by AI-generated insights, so be selective about which metrics and findings align with your product goals.

## 3.  *Design: From Sketches to AI-Powered Prototypes*

When you think of AI, you might not immediately think of design, but AI is transforming this phase, too.

### *AI Tools for Design:*

- **Sketch-to-Code Tools:** Tools like **Uizard, Sketch2Code, and Adobe Sensei** can convert hand-drawn wireframes into digital mockups. This means you can go from concept to prototype in a matter of hours, not days.

- **AI in UX/UI Design:** AI plugins for tools like **Figma** suggest design improvements based on user behavior data, such as button placement, font size, and color schemes. AI tools can also automate A/B testing, showing different designs to user segments and providing data-driven feedback on which design performs better.

🔍 **Example in Action:** Slack's product teams use AI-enhanced design tools to test various layouts and features, making rapid iterations based on user feedback. For instance, they might use AI to analyze how users interact with different layouts in real-time, using heatmaps to identify which parts of the interface attract the most attention.

📌 ***Pro Tip***: Use AI-generated design suggestions as inspiration, not gospel. AI might suggest changes based on statistical data, but the final design decision should be guided by user empathy and brand consistency.

## 4. *Development: AI as Your Coding Partner*

The development phase can be long and arduous, but AI is here to help.

### *AI Tools for Development:*

- **AI-Powered Coding Assistants:** Tools like **GitHub Copilot and Tabnine** predict and complete code as you type, significantly speeding up coding while reducing errors. Imagine having a colleague who knows your coding habits and preferences—it's kind of like that.

- **AI in Testing:** AI-powered testing tools like **ReTest, Test.ai, and Applitools** automate regression testing, finding bugs faster than any human QA could. These tools use machine learning to detect patterns that might indicate code defects or potential crashes.

- **AI in CI/CD Pipelines:** Continuous integration/continuous deployment (CI/CD) is faster with AI. AI can optimize build processes, predict failures, and even automate rollbacks if something goes wrong.

🔍 **Example in Action:** Google's use of AI in project management tools like Asana and Jira goes beyond simple task tracking. AI automates status updates, predicts potential delays, and even assigns tasks based on team members' past performance and current workload.

📌 ***Pro Tip:*** While AI can speed up coding and testing, don't skip manual checks. AI is great at spotting patterns, but it might miss context-specific issues that only a human can identify.

## 5.    *Launch: Real-Time Adaptation with AI*

The launch phase is critical because it's your first chance to see how users interact with the product in the real world.

### *AI Tools for Launch:*

- **AI-Powered Analytics:** Tools like **Mixpanel and Google Analytics 360**[25] offer AI-driven insights into user behavior post-launch. AI analyzes clicks, scrolls, and interactions, helping you identify which features are popular and which need improvement.

- **AI in Customer Feedback Analysis:** Post-launch, tools like **Qualtrics and SurveyMonkey Genius** can analyze customer feedback, identifying common themes and sentiments, which can then be used for real-time product updates[26].

🔍 **Example in Action:** Spotify uses AI during launches to analyze user data and engagement. For instance, when Spotify launched its "Blend" feature, AI was used to

---

[25] Mixpanel and Google Analytics 360 utilize AI algorithms to analyze user behavior, including clicks, scrolls, and interactions. These insights help identify popular features and areas needing improvement, enhancing post-launch optimization strategies Analytify Typedream SkillUpwards

[26] These insights allow for real-time adjustments to product offerings, enhancing user experience and satisfaction Polling.com Business Wire CustomerThink.

identify how users were engaging with it, leading to rapid adjustments based on early user feedback.

📌 *Pro Tip*: Launches are high-stakes moments, but AI helps you stay agile. Use AI data to adapt quickly, but always keep the user's voice at the forefront.

## 6. *Continuous Improvement: The AI-Driven Feedback Loop*

Product development is never truly "done." AI can help you refine, iterate, and innovate continuously.

### *AI Tools for Continuous Improvement:*

- **AI in A/B Testing:** AI-powered A/B testing tools like **Optimizely and VWO** automatically analyze user responses to different versions of your product, helping you refine it based on data-driven insights.

- **Feature Toggles:** AI can assist in rolling out new features to selected user groups, gathering data, and making rapid adjustments based on real user behavior.

🔍 **Example in Action:** Amazon's Alexa team uses AI to analyze user commands and interactions, continuously refining Alexa's understanding and response capabilities based on real-time data. This continuous feedback loop ensures that Alexa improves with every interaction.

📌 *Pro Tip*: AI can provide endless insights, but make sure to prioritize the most impactful changes. It's easy to get caught up in small tweaks, but focus on the big wins that drive the most value for users.

# ⚒ Streamlining Product Development with AI-Powered Tools

Let's face it: product development can feel like navigating a maze with too many twists and turns. One minute you're riding high with a breakthrough idea, and the next you're buried under endless to-do lists, shifting deadlines, and feedback loops. But with AI in the mix, it's like switching from a slow crawl to a rocket ride.

AI-powered product management tools, like **Jira Align** and **Monday.com's** AI features, are the secret sauce for a more efficient process. They don't just help you stay organized—they revolutionize the way you approach development from start to finish. These tools manage tasks, track progress, gather feedback, and even predict potential issues before they become headaches. Imagine an AI assistant whispering in your ear, "Hey, based on the current workload, your prototype launch could be delayed by two weeks. Wanna fix it before it's too late?" It's like having a project manager with superpowers, who never misses a beat and always has your back.

But wait, there's more. These AI tools can also prioritize features based on user feedback, industry trends, and competitor analysis. For example, if customers consistently request a certain feature, AI can help you fast-track it into development, ensuring your product hits the right notes with users. Even better, AI can offer real-time insights into which features are likely to be a hit based on historical data, customer sentiment, and market trends. It's like having a crystal ball that actually works!

Some tools even automate routine tasks, like updating the team on progress or setting up meetings, freeing you up to focus on the creative, strategic parts of product development. They can analyze complex data sets and translate them into simple, actionable insights. No more drowning in spreadsheets or deciphering confusing metrics—AI handles the heavy lifting.

AI doesn't just make you faster; it makes you smarter. By anticipating potential roadblocks, streamlining feedback loops, and prioritizing what really matters, AI turns product development from a chaotic marathon into a well-planned sprint. So, whether you're launching your first product or refining your tenth, AI helps you stay one step ahead, all while making the process feel more manageable and—dare we say it? —a lot more fun.

## ⚙ How Google's AI is Revolutionizing Product Development: Real-World Success Stories

In today's fast-paced digital age, Google stands out as one of the most innovative companies, especially when it comes to leveraging AI to enhance its products. Whether it's improving search accuracy, delivering more relevant ads, or optimizing your daily commute, Google uses AI[27] to ensure its services not only work better but also feel more personalized and useful. Let's take a closer look at how Google incorporates AI into its product development, making our digital experiences smarter, faster, and more tailored to individual needs.

---

[27] Google's AI advancements focus on human-centered design and applications like Google Assistant, Google Photos, and flood prediction tools, emphasizing improved personalization, automation, and disaster management DigitalDefynd People + AI Research HubSpot Blog

## Google Search: Smart, Intuitive Results

When you use Google Search, it's not just about typing in a few words and hoping for the best anymore. The search engine now "understands" what you're looking for, thanks to AI models like BERT (Bidirectional Encoder Representations from Transformers). BERT is like a super-smart assistant that reads your search queries and understands not just the words you type, but the meaning behind them.

Let's say you type, "best hiking trails near me," but you mean trails that are both beginner-friendly and have nice views. Google Search can interpret these nuances, analyzing context like a human might. By constantly processing user queries, BERT and other AI models help Google understand language and intent better, allowing for accurate and context-aware search results that feel more natural and helpful.

## Google Ads: Smarter Ad Delivery for Better Results

If you've ever clicked on an ad that felt weirdly relevant, that's AI at work, too. Google Ads leverages AI to do a lot more than just show random ads. It helps businesses get their ads in front of the right people at the right time. Here's how:

- **Optimized Targeting:** AI analyzes massive datasets to determine who's most likely to click on, engage with, or even purchase from a particular ad. This goes beyond basic demographics like age or location—it looks at behavior, past interactions, and interests to refine ad delivery.

- **Bidding Strategies:** In digital advertising, "bidding" is the process where advertisers compete for ad placement. AI optimizes these bids in real-time, ensuring advertisers don't overspend while still getting their message to the most relevant users.

- **Personalized Ad Placements:** Based on user data, Google can tailor ad placements to appear where they're likely to perform best, like on a user's favorite website or within an app they frequently use.

This AI-driven approach means businesses can see rapid iterations in ad performance, as they get to test what works, adjust quickly, and maximize return on investment (ROI) with data-driven decisions.

## *Google Maps: A Smarter Way to Navigate*

For many of us, Google Maps is more than just a digital map—it's a real-time guide that helps us get where we need to go as quickly and safely as possible. But did you know that AI is the powerhouse behind many of its coolest features?

### *Analyzing Geographic Data for Accurate Traffic Predictions*

Imagine you're rushing to a concert and trying to avoid traffic. Google Maps uses AI to analyze vast geographic datasets, taking into account real-time data from road sensors, historical traffic patterns, and even live user data. This helps it predict traffic congestion and suggest alternative routes almost instantly. AI's ability to process these multiple data sources means that your travel time estimates are continually updated and more accurate.

### *Personalized Recommendations and Real-Time Updates*

Google Maps doesn't just stop at helping you reach your destination; it's also great at personalizing your experience. If you often look for vegetarian restaurants or enjoy hiking trails, Maps will start suggesting these options based on your past searches. AI learns from your preferences and behaviors, making the app feel like it's tailored specifically for you.

### Real-Time Incident Reports

Ever received a notification about an accident ahead or a roadblock before you even see it? That's AI at play again. Google Maps uses AI to aggregate user-reported incidents and other data sources, providing real-time updates that keep you informed of any changes along your route.

### Adding New Features

AI doesn't just make existing features smarter; it also enables Google to add new ones quickly. For example, Maps recently introduced features like more precise Estimated Time of Arrival (ETA) and eco-friendly route options, made possible by analyzing large-scale data patterns and user behavior.

## The Bigger Picture: AI as the Ultimate Innovation Engine at Google

What sets Google apart is not just its use of AI, but how it uses AI to rapidly iterate, improve, and even introduce entirely new features. AI drives Google's ability to test, learn, and adapt quickly. From personalized recommendations in Maps to smarter ad placements that help businesses grow, AI enables Google's products to evolve in real-time, staying ahead of user needs and market demands.

So, next time you use Google's products, think of the AI working tirelessly behind the scenes—an intelligent, evolving force that's making your digital world more efficient, personalized, and just plain easier to navigate.

 # What We Learnt

- **AI is your product development copilot:** It's not just about automation; AI helps you work smarter, offering deeper insights, quicker iterations, and personalized user experiences.

- **Speed + Quality:** AI speeds up repetitive tasks while improving quality. From idea generation to launch, it helps you move faster without compromising on accuracy or creativity.

- **Research made easy:** AI analyzes massive datasets, scans user feedback, and identifies trends—so you know what's working, what's missing, and what's next.

- **Better design and development:** AI can transform rough sketches into prototypes, enhance UI/UX, and make coding/testing faster and more reliable.

- **Improved product development**: AI-powered tools streamline the product development process by managing tasks, predicting issues, and prioritizing features based on feedback and trends.

- **Personalization is key:** Whether it's Netflix's recommendations or Amazon's product suggestions, AI keeps users engaged by creating experiences tailored just for them.

- **It's a continuous improvement loop:** AI doesn't stop at launch. It helps refine, iterate, and improve products based on real-time user feedback and data analysis.

- **Real-world impact:** Google has shown that AI isn't just a fancy add-on; it's a core part of their product strategy, driving innovation and user satisfaction.

# PART 4

## SCALING CAREER GROWTH
## IN THE AGE OF AI

# CHAPTER 9
# DEVELOPING TECHNICAL FLUENCY

Product managers (PMs) today have a powerful tool at their disposal: artificial intelligence (AI). Whether you're building chatbots that improve customer service or recommendation systems that personalize shopping experiences, AI is increasingly becoming central to product management. However, for many PMs, AI can feel daunting—full of complex algorithms, coding languages, and technical jargon. But here's the good news: **you don't need to be a coder to manage AI projects effectively**. Instead, you need to develop a level of technical fluency that allows you to understand

AI concepts, ask the right questions, and make informed decisions that benefit both the product and its users.

This chapter will walk you through the essential aspects of technical fluency for managing AI product development. We'll break down key AI concepts, offer examples of real-world applications, and provide tips on communicating effectively with engineers. Think of this chapter as your AI starter kit—a resource to help you confidently lead AI initiatives without having to dive deep into coding.

# 📖 Why Technical Fluency Matters in AI Product Management

Imagine you're managing a product that uses AI to personalize user recommendations. You know that using machine learning algorithms can help improve accuracy, but what's your role in this process? Do you need to code the model yourself? Definitely not. However, you do need to understand how the model works, the type of data it needs, and what metrics define its success.

Technical fluency helps PMs play an active role in:

- **Strategic decision-making:** By understanding AI concepts, you can decide whether AI is the right solution for your problem and how it aligns with broader business goals.

- **Managing trade-offs:** In AI projects, you'll often need to balance model accuracy, speed, cost, and user experience. Technical knowledge allows you to make informed choices when deciding between different options.

- **Facilitating communication:** Knowing enough about AI helps you ask better questions, provide clear feedback, and effectively collaborate with engineers, designers, and stakeholders.

- **Ensuring ethical AI use:** AI can amplify biases if not managed carefully. With technical fluency, you can identify potential biases and work toward creating fair, transparent AI systems.

The AI product landscape is fast-paced and ever-evolving. Gaining technical fluency ensures you can keep up with changes, explore new possibilities, and guide your teams toward innovative solutions.

# 📖 Communicating with Engineers Without Being a Coder

Effective communication is at the heart of successful product management. But when the technical side of things, especially in AI projects, seems more like rocket science than a coffee chat, it's easy to feel overwhelmed. The good news? You don't need to become a coding wizard to connect meaningfully with engineers. Here's how you can build a bridge between tech talk and PM strategy—without any late-night programming classes.

## *1.    Embrace a Growth Mindset*

First, approach AI like your favorite Netflix series—one episode at a time. The world of AI is like an ever-expanding universe: it's fast-paced, intriguing, and often full of twists. So, be curious. Let yourself explore new concepts, read articles, or attend AI-focused webinars when you can. You don't need to become the next AI guru, but a bit of enthusiasm for learning can go a long way. Be the PM who's not afraid to say, "Hey, I'm still learning this, but I'd love to understand it better!"

## 2. *Simplify AI Concepts with Analogies*

If AI jargon makes you feel like you're trying to understand the fine print of a rental car agreement, you're not alone. Analogies can be your secret weapon for untangling those technical terms. Here are a few to keep handy:

- **"Training a Model"** is like teaching a puppy to do tricks. You start by showing it simple commands (like data), reward it when it gets it right, and keep repeating until it learns the pattern. Sometimes it'll make mistakes, but that's part of the learning curve.

- **"Data Pipelines"** are like making your morning coffee. Raw data is like coffee beans—you need to grind, brew, and maybe add some milk and sugar before you have the final product: a robust AI model ready to deliver results.

- **"Model Drift"** is like having a GPS that slowly gets worse at giving directions. Over time, models can lose accuracy, just like a GPS that hasn't been updated with new roads.

By translating complex AI concepts into relatable analogies, you're not only able to understand them better, but you can also communicate them more clearly to other stakeholders, like marketing or sales teams.

## 3. *Use User Stories to Drive Communication*

User stories aren't just for developers; they're a universal language for aligning everyone's understanding. Writing user stories for AI products involves a bit more nuance since AI can be unpredictable. So, the clearer you are about the intended outcomes, the better.

### 🔍 *For example:*

- "As a customer service representative, I want the AI chatbot to provide quick, relevant responses so I can resolve customer issues efficiently."

- "As a user, I want the AI-based recommendation system to consider my recent purchases, so I get suggestions that align with my interests."

These stories help engineers grasp the end user's needs and goals while reminding everyone of the broader vision. It's less about the code itself and more about the purpose behind it.

## 4.    *Create a Culture of Open Dialogue*

Let's be honest: nobody likes feeling dumb. So, foster a culture where engineers feel comfortable breaking things down for non-technical folks. In team meetings, encourage engineers to use plain language. You can even frame questions like this:

- "How would you explain this to someone without an engineering background?"

- "If this AI feature were a feature in a popular app, which one would it be and why?"

Encouraging engineers to explain things in a simpler way benefits everyone. It helps PMs understand the tech better and gives engineers a chance to reframe their work in a new light. Plus, it just makes for a more collaborative, friendly work environment.

## 5. *Use Visual Tools to Communicate AI Workflows*

Diagrams, flowcharts, and visual dashboards can transform abstract concepts into clear, tangible ideas. Tools like Lucidchart, Miro, or even a good ol' whiteboard can be your allies here. Visual tools can help map out:

- **Data Pipelines:** Show the journey of data from raw input to AI-ready format.

- **Model Architectures:** Depict how data flows through different layers of an AI model.

- **AI Dashboards:** Display key metrics that allow you to monitor the AI's performance in real-time.

Even if you're not creating these visuals yourself, requesting them from engineers can help foster clarity for everyone.

## 6. *Be Comfortable with Not Knowing Everything*

It's okay to admit that some AI topics are a bit beyond your expertise. What matters is your willingness to learn and your genuine interest in helping the team succeed. Saying, "I'm not sure, but I'd love to learn more" is not a sign of weakness—it's a mark of a strong, open-minded PM.

Communicating with engineers as a PM doesn't mean you need to speak code fluently. It's more about understanding the language of collaboration and making complex topics relatable. The key is to stay curious, use analogies, write clear user stories, foster open dialogue, and embrace visual aids. You may not be a coder, but you can still be the glue that holds the team together. And who knows? You might even find yourself enjoying AI jargon... well, maybe a little!

# Key Areas of Technical Fluency

To effectively manage AI products, PMs need a good grasp of several core areas of AI. Here, we'll dive deep into each key area, providing detailed insights that can help you navigate AI projects with confidence.

## *1.  Understanding Data Models and Pipelines*

Data models and pipelines are fundamental to AI product development. Here's what you need to know:

- **Data Pipelines:** These are the processes through which raw data is collected, cleaned, transformed, and loaded into AI models. A typical pipeline involves:

    o **Data collection:** Gathering relevant data from various sources.

    o **Data cleaning:** Removing inconsistencies, duplicates, and errors.

    o **Data transformation:** Converting data into a format that AI models can process.

    o **Feature engineering:** Identifying and creating relevant features that will help the model learn patterns effectively.

- **Data Models:** AI models rely on data to learn. As a PM, you need to understand different types of data models:

    o **Structured Data Models:** Work with well-organized data (e.g., spreadsheets, databases).

    o **Unstructured Data Models:** Handle data like images, text, or videos.

○ **Deep Learning Models:** Use neural networks to process large amounts of data, often found in applications like computer vision or NLP.

🔍 *Example:* Suppose you're building a fraud detection system for a bank. You'll need a data pipeline that collects transaction data, cleans it for inaccuracies, and then feeds it into a supervised learning model trained to identify suspicious patterns. As the PM, you need to understand these steps conceptually, so you can align them with product goals and user needs.

## 2. *Machine Learning Algorithms: Types and Use Cases*

Machine learning (ML) is the engine behind most AI projects. There are several types of ML algorithms, each suited to different tasks:

- **Supervised Learning:** These algorithms are trained using labeled data (i.e., data where the outcome is already known). Common use cases include:

  ○ **Regression models:** Predicting numerical values (e.g., sales forecasting).

  ○ **Classification models:** Categorizing data into predefined classes (e.g., spam detection).

- **Unsupervised Learning:** Used when data is unlabeled, helping AI identify patterns or clusters within the data. Common applications include:

  ○ **Clustering algorithms:** Grouping similar data points together (e.g., customer segmentation).

○ **Dimensionality reduction:** Simplifying complex data sets while retaining key information.

- **Reinforcement Learning (RL):** RL algorithms learn through trial and error, receiving feedback from their actions. It's like training a dog with treats; the AI "learns" from rewards. Common use cases include:

    ○ **Gaming:** AI bots learning to play games like chess or Go.

    ○ **Robotics:** AI guiding robots to complete tasks like navigation or object manipulation.

🔍 *Example:* IBM Watson's product managers[28] collaborate with engineers to tailor supervised learning algorithms for applications like customer service chatbots. These chatbots are trained to recognize customer intent based on labeled training data (e.g., user queries categorized by intent).

## 3. *Natural Language Processing (NLP)*

Natural Language Processing (NLP) is a vital AI domain that focuses on enabling machines to understand, interpret, and respond to human language. Key concepts to know include:

- **Tokenization:** Breaking down text into smaller units (words or sentences) that the AI can process.

---

[28] IBM Watson's product management approach emphasizes close collaboration between product managers (PMs) and engineers to design and refine AI applications like customer service chatbots. https://digitaldefynd.com/IQ/ai-in-product-development-case-studies/

- **Sentiment Analysis:** Identifying the sentiment (positive, negative, neutral) behind text inputs.

- **Named Entity Recognition (NER):** Identifying and categorizing entities in text (e.g., names, locations, dates).

- **Language Generation:** Enabling AI to generate human-like responses or content.

🔍 *Example:* IBM Watson's NLP capabilities help healthcare providers analyze medical notes for important information like symptoms or diagnoses. Product managers working with Watson don't need to understand the complex algorithms behind NLP but must know how to align NLP capabilities with specific business goals, like improving diagnostic accuracy.

## 4. *Model Evaluation, Testing, and Metrics*

Evaluation is a critical part of the AI development process, as it ensures that models meet the intended business outcomes. Here's how PMs can understand AI model evaluation:

### *Key Metrics:*

- **Accuracy:** Percentage of correct predictions made by the model.

- **Precision:** Measures how many of the positive predictions are actually correct.

- **Recall:** Measures how many actual positives were correctly identified by the model.

- **F1-Score:** Balances precision and recall, useful when you need to consider both metrics simultaneously.

🔍 *Example:* If you're managing a recommendation system, high precision means the AI is good at recommending the right products to users, but low recall could indicate that it's missing out on some potential matches. As a PM, you'll need to decide whether to prioritize precision (relevance) or recall (coverage) based on user feedback and business objectives.

## 5. Ethics, Fairness, and Bias in AI

Ethics in AI isn't just a buzzword—it's a crucial component of responsible AI management. As a PM, you should be aware of potential ethical pitfalls:

- **Bias in Data:** AI models learn from historical data, which can include biases. For example, an AI hiring system trained on past hiring data might favor certain demographics over others if biases existed in the original data.

- **Explainability:** Ensure AI models are interpretable. This means having the ability to explain how the AI makes its decisions to users and stakeholders.

- **Fairness and Transparency:** Make sure your AI models treat all users fairly and transparently. This might involve testing models for bias and ensuring that sensitive variables (e.g., race, gender) don't affect outcomes unfairly.

🔍 *Example:* IBM's Watson PMs work to ensure that the AI models used in healthcare applications do not introduce biases that could affect patient care. They collaborate with data scientists to identify and address potential biases in training data, ensuring that models are fair and effective.

# 📖 Resources for Learning AI and Data Science Fundamentals

To develop technical fluency, PMs should continuously learn and adapt. Here's a deep dive into resources that can help:

## 1. *Online Courses and Tutorials*

- **Coursera:** Offers AI courses like "AI for Everyone" by Andrew Ng, providing a broad overview of AI concepts, terminology, and ethical considerations.

- **Udemy:** Features beginner-friendly courses that cover machine learning fundamentals, practical coding exercises, and real-world AI applications.

- **Khan Academy:** A great resource for foundational math, statistics, and probability—essential for understanding AI models.

## 2. *Books for In-Depth Knowledge*

- **"The Hundred-Page Machine Learning Book" by Andriy Burkov:** This book offers a concise yet comprehensive overview of machine learning concepts, written for non-technical readers.

- **"Prediction Machines" by Ajay Agrawal, Joshua Gans, and Avi Goldfarb:** Provides insights into how AI makes predictions and impacts business strategies.

## 3. *Podcasts, Videos, and Webinars*

- **"Data Skeptic" Podcast:** Breaks down complex AI topics into digestible episodes, covering everything from NLP to deep learning.

- **YouTube Channels:** Channels like "Two Minute Papers" simplify AI research papers, helping you understand cutting-edge AI developments in a few minutes.

### 4.   *AI Meetups, Hackathons, and Conferences*

- Join local AI meetups or attend virtual hackathons to see AI solutions in action and network with AI practitioners.

- Attend AI-focused conferences like "The Ai4 Conference" or "AI Summit" to learn from experts and discover industry trends.

### 5.   *AI Communities and Forums*

- Engage with communities on **LinkedIn**, **Stack Overflow**, and **Reddit** (e.g., r/MachineLearning)[29]. These platforms offer discussions, expert insights, and answers to AI-related questions.

# 🔍 Real-World Example: IBM Watson Product Managers

IBM Watson's product managers (PMs) offer a compelling blueprint for managing AI projects effectively. Watson, IBM's flagship AI product, leverages advanced natural language processing (NLP) and machine learning to deliver solutions in diverse industries, including healthcare, finance, and customer service. Watson's PMs play a crucial role in aligning AI capabilities with business goals, often acting as the bridge between AI engineers

---

[29] Engaging with online communities like LinkedIn, Stack Overflow, and Reddit (e.g., r/MachineLearning) can be highly beneficial for staying updated on AI topics. For further exploration, see sources like U.OSU r/MachineLearning on Reddit.

and business stakeholders. Let's delve into how they navigate this process, the strategies they employ, and some practical tips that you can apply to your own AI product management efforts.

## 1. *Understanding AI's Business Potential Across Industries*

Watson PMs are adept at identifying how AI can address specific challenges within different industries. Their role involves a deep understanding of industry pain points and user needs. For instance:

- **In Healthcare:** Watson's AI models are designed to analyze large volumes of unstructured medical data, such as electronic health records (EHRs), research papers, and medical notes. Watson PMs collaborate with data scientists to develop models that help doctors make more informed decisions about patient diagnoses and treatment plans. They align AI capabilities with the industry's needs by focusing on improving patient outcomes, reducing diagnostic errors, and streamlining administrative tasks.

- **In Finance:** AI models are used for fraud detection, compliance, and customer service in banking. Watson PMs work with engineers to train models that can analyze transactional data to identify potential fraud in real-time. They ensure that AI is implemented in a way that minimizes false positives while maintaining robust detection capabilities, enabling financial institutions to enhance both security and customer trust.

- **In Customer Service:** Watson PMs develop AI-driven chatbots and virtual assistants to improve user experiences. These AI tools use NLP to understand customer queries and provide relevant responses. For instance, a customer service chatbot might help resolve billing issues, provide product recommendations, or answer frequently asked questions.

## 2. *Developing AI Strategies Aligned with User Needs*

Watson PMs don't just focus on the technical aspects; they emphasize user-centric design in AI solutions. This means understanding the end-user's challenges, needs, and expectations before shaping AI functionalities. Here's how they achieve that alignment:

- **User Research & Interviews:** Watson PMs frequently engage with industry experts, end-users, and key stakeholders to understand specific pain points and opportunities for AI. For example, before developing a clinical decision support system, PMs might interview doctors to understand the type of information they need quickly during patient consultations.

- **Defining AI Use Cases Clearly:** Watson PMs articulate use cases in a way that highlights the value AI can provide. Instead of saying, "We're using NLP to analyze medical records," they frame it as, "Our AI solution will help doctors quickly identify potential diagnoses by summarizing patient history and recent lab results, reducing manual effort."

- **Validating Hypotheses:** Before deploying AI models on a large scale, Watson PMs validate hypotheses through pilot testing and small-scale rollouts. For example, they might test an AI recommendation engine with a small group of users to ensure that it delivers relevant suggestions before scaling up.

## 3. *Engaging in Continuous Learning*

AI technologies evolve rapidly, and Watson PMs stay ahead by constantly updating their technical knowledge. Here's how they maintain their technical fluency:

- **Internal Training Programs:** Watson offers internal training programs, workshops, and seminars where PMs can learn about the latest AI tools, algorithms, and ethical considerations. PMs actively participate in these sessions to understand the technical intricacies of AI and how they relate to product strategy.

- **Cross-Functional Collaboration:** Watson PMs frequently collaborate with data scientists, AI researchers, engineers, and industry specialists. They observe engineers during model training sessions, ask questions about algorithm performance, and engage in discussions about model accuracy, recall, and F1-scores. By being present in these technical conversations, they enhance their understanding of AI's inner workings.

- **Staying Updated on AI Trends:** Watson PMs also invest time in reading AI research papers, attending AI conferences, and following thought leaders in the AI space. This helps them identify emerging trends and potential AI applications that could offer a competitive advantage.

## What We Learnt

- **AI Product Management Doesn't Require Coding:** You don't have to write code, but understanding AI concepts and workflows is essential for effective product management.

- **Effective Communication with Engineers:** Use analogies, simplify technical terms, and craft clear user stories to bridge the gap between business needs and AI solutions.

- **Key AI Concepts to Know:** Understand the basics of data pipelines, machine learning models, natural language processing (NLP), and AI evaluation metrics like accuracy, precision, recall, and F1-score.

- **Continuous Learning is Essential:** AI changes rapidly, so make it a habit to explore new trends, research, and events to maintain your technical fluency.

- **Ethics First:** Always prioritize ethical AI by addressing biases, ensuring transparency, and focusing on fair decision-making.

- **Resources are Your Best Friend:** Take advantage of online courses, podcasts, and AI communities to enhance your knowledge in a way that suits your learning style.

- **Real-World Example of IBM Watson:** Watson PMs successfully align AI capabilities with business goals across industries by focusing on user needs.

- **The Core Lesson:** Technical fluency is about asking the right questions, understanding AI's potential, and aligning it with your product strategy, rather than mastering coding skills.

# CHAPTER 10
# LEVERAGING AI FOR DECISION-MAKING

AI's integration into business processes has shifted decision-making from intuition-based to data-driven, allowing product managers to confidently navigate complex markets and consumer demands. This chapter will dive into how AI serves as a valuable tool in the decision-making arsenal, enabling more precise strategies and effective solutions.

For product managers—especially those who are tech-savvy and keen on innovation—AI offers a significant edge. From analyzing customer behavior to predicting future trends, AI supports critical decisions that can make or break a product's success. Let's explore the practical ways AI can help make more informed decisions, with a specific example of how Coca-Cola has leveraged AI for product innovation.

## 📖 The Role of AI in Enhancing Decision-Making

AI supports product managers in various ways:

### 1.   Consumer Insights & Behavioral Analytics

Product managers thrive on understanding their target audience, but the sheer volume of consumer data today is overwhelming. AI can sift through this data quickly, identifying patterns in consumer preferences and behaviors. This data is often collected from:

- Social media platforms

- Online customer reviews

- E-commerce sites

- CRM (Customer Relationship Management) databases

AI doesn't just look at what consumers are buying; it digs into *why* they're buying. By analyzing this data, AI can help product managers understand the underlying motivations, values, and preferences of their audience.

For instance, AI tools can analyze customer feedback and cluster it into themes like "positive sentiment," "negative sentiment," "product design issues," or "shipping complaints." This categorization enables product managers to prioritize areas of improvement that matter most to consumers. Moreover, these insights can also help tailor marketing campaigns, personalize user experiences, and ultimately drive better engagement and sales.

## 2.    *Predictive Analytics for Trend Forecasting*

Predictive analytics is one of AI's most impactful applications for product managers. It uses historical data to forecast future outcomes, making it easier to anticipate market trends, consumer demand, and even potential risks.

For product managers, predictive analytics can be the difference between launching a hit product and watching it flop. It enables teams to:

- **Anticipate seasonal demand:** AI can analyze historical sales data to forecast demand for specific products during certain times of the year.

- **Identify emerging trends:** By analyzing social media trends and online searches, AI can help detect new consumer preferences or niche markets that might be worth pursuing.

- **Optimize inventory levels:** Predictive analytics can also forecast demand more accurately, reducing the risk of overstocking or understocking.

## 3. *Enhanced Product Development*

AI is also transforming how product managers approach product development. With AI-powered analytics, teams can identify which features or attributes are most likely to resonate with consumers, even before the product is developed.

For example, Coca-Cola's use of AI to develop new flavors isn't just about identifying popular tastes; it's about understanding *why* certain flavors resonate. AI can analyze consumer preferences based on cultural trends, regional tastes, and even emotional responses. This data-driven approach allows product managers to create products that align more closely with consumer expectations.

Additionally, AI can help streamline product testing and iteration. Tools like A/B testing, sentiment analysis, and virtual prototyping allow teams to gather real-time feedback and adjust product features accordingly. This rapid feedback loop accelerates the product development cycle, enabling faster iterations and better final products.

## 4.    *Real-time Data Analysis for Agile Decision-Making*

Gone are the days when product managers relied solely on quarterly reports and annual reviews. Today, decisions need to be made in real-time, and AI facilitates this agile decision-making process. AI tools can analyze data in real-time, providing product managers with instant insights that can guide decisions on the fly.

For example, AI-powered dashboards can provide live updates on sales performance, social media engagement, and customer feedback. If a new flavor launch isn't performing as expected, AI can help diagnose the issue—whether it's related to marketing, distribution, or the product itself. This level of agility is crucial for product managers who need to pivot quickly and respond to market changes.

## 5.    *Personalization at Scale*

One of AI's greatest strengths is its ability to personalize experiences at scale. Whether it's customizing website experiences, tailoring marketing messages, or recommending products, AI enables product managers to create individualized experiences for thousands, if not millions, of consumers.

# 🔍 Example: Coca-Cola Uses AI-Driven Analytics to Determine New Flavors

Coca-Cola, a brand synonymous with innovation, has always been at the forefront of leveraging emerging technologies. In recent years, the company has harnessed AI-driven analytics to refine its product offerings and stay ahead in the beverage industry[30]. Let's dive into this example in detail, as it perfectly encapsulates how AI can be used to make strategic, data-backed decisions in product management.

## 1. *Understanding the Problem: How to Decide on New Flavors*

For a global beverage brand like Coca-Cola, deciding which flavors to introduce is a high-stakes challenge. The market is highly competitive, consumer tastes are constantly evolving, and there's a need to align new flavors with regional preferences while also maintaining brand consistency. Traditionally, flavor decisions relied on market research, consumer surveys, and feedback from focus groups. However, this approach has limitations:

- Biases in survey responses

- Small sample sizes, leading to skewed data

- Longer time frames to gather insights and act upon them

In an industry where timing is critical, Coca-Cola needed a faster, more reliable way to analyze vast amounts of consumer data. This is where AI stepped in as a key player.

---

[30] Coca-Cola has successfully integrated AI-driven analytics into its product development strategy, particularly in creating new flavors. For instance, the company introduced Y3000 Zero Sugar, a flavor co-created with AI that uses consumer feedback and cultural insights to predict preferences. AI tools were used to analyze customer interactions, social media data, and market trends to generate this futuristic flavor, highlighting the role of AI in both flavor innovation and strategic decision-making. https://aromatechgroup.com/actus-business-units/ai-the-new-flavor-maker/

## 2.    *AI-Driven Analytics: How Coca-Cola Applied AI to Decision-Making*

Coca-Cola implemented AI-driven analytics tools that could process vast amounts of consumer data in real-time. This data included social media trends, sales data, consumer reviews, and regional market preferences. Here's how AI helped in the decision-making process:

### *Collecting Data from Multiple Sources*

AI systems gathered information from various sources, including:

- **Social media platforms:** AI tools used sentiment analysis to track conversations about Coca-Cola products, competitors' products, and emerging beverage trends.

- **Sales databases:** By examining historical sales data, AI identified patterns in consumer buying behavior—such as increased interest in citrus flavors during summer months or preferences for lower-sugar drinks in health-conscious markets.

- **Customer feedback platforms:** AI combed through product reviews and feedback forms to detect recurring themes, such as "desire for more exotic flavors" or "preference for zero-sugar options."

This holistic data collection provided a more comprehensive view of consumer preferences.

### *Analyzing Consumer Trends and Predicting Flavors*

Once the data was collected, AI algorithms analyzed the trends to predict which flavors would have the highest likelihood of success. The AI models considered factors like:

- **Seasonal demand patterns:** AI detected spikes in interest for certain ingredients, like mango or ginger, during specific times of the year.

- **Regional preferences:** AI identified variations in taste across different geographies—e.g., consumers in South Asia leaning towards spicy or tangy flavors, while those in North America favored sweeter or fruit-based options.

- **Health trends:** AI also flagged a growing demand for healthier, low-calorie beverages, pushing product managers to focus more on flavors that could be paired with zero-calorie sweeteners.

## *Making Informed Decisions*

With these insights, Coca-Cola's product managers had the data to back up their decisions. Instead of relying on intuition or traditional market research alone, they could now pinpoint which flavors would likely resonate with different consumer segments. This data-driven approach helped in:

- **Faster decision-making:** AI reduced the time needed to identify emerging flavor trends.

- **Higher confidence in choices:** Product managers felt more assured that their decisions were backed by solid data, reducing the risk of product failures.

- **Effective product launches:** AI insights informed everything from flavor development to marketing strategies, ensuring that new products were aligned with consumer desires.

## 3.  The Broader Benefits of AI in Decision-Making

While Coca-Cola's use of AI to identify new flavors is just one example, the broader benefits of AI in decision-making are significant. Here are a few key advantages:

### Speed and Efficiency

AI operates 24/7, processing large datasets in a fraction of the time it would take humans. This leads to quicker decision-making, which is especially beneficial in competitive markets where timing is critical.

### Eliminating Human Bias

Traditional decision-making can be influenced by personal biases, subjective opinions, or limited data access. AI minimizes these biases by providing objective insights based on large, diverse datasets.

### Improved Accuracy and Precision

AI algorithms excel at detecting patterns and correlations that might be missed by human analysts. This precision allows for more accurate predictions and, consequently, better decision-making outcomes.

### Enhanced Personalization

AI can also be used to tailor decisions to specific consumer segments. For example, AI can segment audiences based on preferences, demographics, and behaviors, allowing product managers to create products that are more personalized and likely to succeed in targeted markets.

## Cost Reduction

By reducing the need for extensive manual research, AI can help lower costs associated with product development, market research, and consumer testing.

## 4.    *Applying AI in Your Role as a Product Manager*

If you're a product manager looking to leverage AI for decision-making, here are practical steps to get started:

### Familiarize Yourself with AI Tools

There are various AI tools designed for product management, from analytics platforms to natural language processing (NLP) tools that can analyze customer feedback. Invest time in understanding which tools align best with your specific needs.

### Start Small but Scale Gradually

It's best to start with smaller projects, such as using AI for customer sentiment analysis or trend predictions. Once you're comfortable, you can expand AI usage to more complex areas like sales forecasting or product launch strategies.

### Collaborate with Data Scientists

Work closely with data scientists or AI specialists within your organization to understand how AI models are developed, tested, and deployed. This will give you a clearer idea of the potential and limitations of AI in decision-making.

### Stay Updated on AI Trends

The AI landscape is continuously evolving, with new technologies emerging regularly. Stay informed about the latest trends and advancements to ensure that you're using cutting-edge tools in your decision-making processes.

## 5. *Future Prospects: AI's Role in Product Innovation*

AI's role in decision-making will only grow more integral as technology evolves. In the near future, AI could enable even more sophisticated applications, such as:

- **Real-time product testing:** AI could predict consumer reactions to new flavors or products before they even hit the shelves.

- **Dynamic pricing models:** AI could set optimal pricing based on demand, competition, and consumer behavior, further enhancing decision-making.

- **Hyper-personalized product messaging:** AI could refine marketing strategies to the individual level, ensuring higher engagement and conversion rates.

The possibilities are virtually endless, but one thing is clear: AI will continue to shape how product managers make decisions, innovate products, and deliver value to consumers.

## *Conclusion*

AI isn't just a tool for automation; it's a strategic asset that helps product managers make better, faster, and more informed decisions. Coca-Cola's experience with AI-driven flavor development is a testament to AI's potential in decision-making. By integrating AI into your decision-making processes, you can not only keep pace with the market but also anticipate its next moves. In a world where consumer tastes change rapidly, AI offers the insights needed to stay ahead.

 **What We Learnt**

- **AI transforms decision-making** by shifting it from intuition-based to data-driven, enhancing accuracy and speed.

- **AI-driven analytics** can help product managers identify emerging trends, preferences, and consumer behavior, enabling faster, more precise product innovations.

- **AI reduces human biases** in decision-making by analyzing large datasets objectively.

- **Real-world example:** Coca-Cola successfully used AI to analyze consumer data, identify flavor trends, and guide product launches, demonstrating AI's practical application in product management.

- **AI offers broader benefits** like improved efficiency, reduced costs, and the ability to segment and personalize products for different consumer groups.

- **Steps for product managers:** Familiarize with AI tools, start small and scale gradually, collaborate with data experts, and stay updated on AI advancements.

- **Future potential:** AI's role in decision-making will expand, offering opportunities in real-time product testing, dynamic pricing, and hyper-personalized marketing.

# CHAPTER 11
# AI AND CAREER GROWTH
# IN PRODUCT MANAGEMENT

## 📖 Embracing AI for Career Growth

In today's rapidly evolving digital landscape, product management is no longer just about managing features or timelines—it's about mastering emerging technologies that shape the future of industries. Artificial Intelligence (AI) is at the forefront of this transformation, redefining how products are conceived, developed, and delivered. For Gen Z, the tech-savvy generation entering the workforce, this shift presents a unique opportunity. As a product manager, leveraging AI can significantly accelerate your career growth and establish you as a forward-thinking leader in your field.

The goal of this chapter is simple: provide you with practical steps and strategies to integrate AI into your career toolkit, so you can thrive in AI-driven product management roles. Whether you're just starting your career or looking to advance to the next level, understanding AI can be the game-changer that sets you apart.

## 📖 AI as a Differentiator in Career Growth for Product Managers

AI is no longer a buzzword—it's a necessity for any product manager looking to excel. Companies across industries are prioritizing AI integration to enhance user experiences, optimize processes, and improve decision-making. The result? An increased demand for product managers who not only understand AI but can also strategically apply it.

## 1. *Why AI Matters for Product Managers*

AI isn't just about automating tasks; it's about enabling smarter decision-making, personalizing user experiences, and anticipating customer needs. As a product manager, here's how AI can act as a differentiator:

- **Enhanced Decision-Making:** AI can process vast amounts of data and identify patterns that may be missed by human analysis alone. As a product manager, this means you can make informed decisions faster and with greater accuracy, boosting your credibility among stakeholders.

- **Personalized User Experiences:** AI-driven features, such as recommendation engines and chatbots, can create tailored experiences that increase user engagement and satisfaction. Building products with such capabilities can distinguish you as an innovative product manager who understands the nuances of user-centric design.

- **Predictive Insights:** AI models can forecast user behavior, market trends, and potential issues, giving you a proactive edge in planning product strategies. Imagine being the product manager who accurately predicts a customer need before it becomes a widespread demand—that's the kind of career-defining impact AI can have.

AI doesn't just streamline processes; it amplifies the value you bring as a product manager, helping you stand out in a competitive job market.

## 2. *How AI Changes the Product Development Process*

The traditional product development cycle—conceptualization, design, development, and launch—gets a significant boost with AI integration:

- **Data-Driven Ideation:** AI tools like natural language processing (NLP) can analyze user feedback, market research, and competitor reviews to identify unmet needs or gaps in the market. As a product manager, you can leverage these insights to pitch new ideas or refine existing ones.

- **Automated Design and Prototyping:** AI can assist with everything from wireframing to prototyping. For instance, tools like Framer or Uizard use AI to suggest design layouts based on user behavior data. This means you can prototype faster and gather feedback sooner.

- **Iterative Development with AI Feedback Loops:** Once a product is live, AI tools can help you monitor user interactions and gather insights in real-time. Tools like Mixpanel and Amplitude use AI to provide data on user flows and friction points, enabling you to iterate quickly and improve user experiences.

- **AI-Powered Testing and Quality Assurance:** AI-driven testing tools can simulate thousands of user scenarios, reducing the time needed for QA and ensuring more robust products. This enables product managers to focus on strategy and user experience rather than getting bogged down in testing details.

AI makes product development faster, smarter, and more aligned with user needs. As you become adept at integrating AI into the product development lifecycle, you'll establish yourself as a tech-savvy, innovative leader capable of driving impactful change.

# 📖 Leveraging AI Certifications and Credentials to Stand Out

In a field that's constantly evolving, credentials can be a game-changer. While hands-on experience remains essential, having AI certifications signals to employers and peers that you're committed to staying at the forefront of technology. Let's explore how to strategically pursue and leverage AI-related credentials.

## *1.   The Value of AI Certifications*

Certifications provide structured learning, industry recognition, and proof of your skills. While they don't replace practical experience, they offer several advantages:

- **Structured Learning Path:** AI certifications guide you through a structured learning process, ensuring you cover essential topics like machine learning (ML), natural language processing (NLP), data analytics, and AI ethics.

- **Industry Validation:** Holding certifications from reputable organizations (e.g., Google, IBM, Coursera, or Stanford) adds credibility to your resume. It signals that you have verified skills and understand AI fundamentals, which can be especially useful when applying for AI-focused product roles.

- **Increased Confidence:** Earning a certification not only improves your technical knowledge but also boosts your confidence in discussions about AI. This can be particularly useful during interviews or stakeholder meetings where technical expertise is crucial.

## 2. *Recommended AI Certifications for Product Managers*

Here's a curated list of some of the most relevant AI certifications for product managers:

- **IBM's Applied AI Professional Certificate:** This program is designed for those looking to gain hands-on AI experience. It covers topics like ML algorithms, data science tools, and AI applications across industries.

- **Coursera's AI for Everyone by Andrew Ng:** A great starting point for understanding AI concepts, this course is designed for non-technical professionals. It provides an overview of AI technologies and their business applications.

- **DataCamp's Machine Learning for Product Managers:** This course bridges the gap between ML concepts and product management. It covers how to use ML in product strategy, user research, and iterative development.

## 3. *How to Choose the Right Certification?*

Not all certifications are created equal, so choosing the right one is critical. Consider the following factors:

- **Relevance to Your Role:** Opt for certifications that align with your current or desired role. If you're already a product manager, go for courses that focus on the application of AI in product management rather than purely technical coding skills.

- **Learning Style:** Some certifications are highly technical and hands-on, while others focus more on strategic applications of AI. Choose one that matches your learning style and career goals.

- **Industry Recognition:** Prioritize certifications from well-known institutions, as they carry more weight with employers and add credibility to your LinkedIn profile or resume.

Completing these certifications can fast-track your AI learning curve, making you more competitive and demonstrating a commitment to continuous learning—an essential trait in AI-driven roles.

# 📖 Building a Personal Brand as an AI-Savvy Product Manager

While certifications and technical skills are essential, they're only part of the equation. Building a personal brand around your AI expertise can amplify your career growth, open doors to new opportunities, and establish you as a thought leader in the product management space.

## 1. *Why Personal Branding Matters*

Personal branding is about showcasing your unique value proposition. It's how you communicate your skills, experiences, and perspectives to the world. Here's why it's crucial for AI-driven product managers:

- **Increased Visibility:** A strong personal brand makes you more visible to recruiters, potential collaborators, and industry leaders. It can lead to job offers, speaking engagements, and collaboration opportunities.

- **Credibility and Trust:** By sharing your insights and successes in AI integration, you establish credibility within your network. People begin to trust your opinions on AI-related topics, which can boost your influence in meetings, negotiations, and strategic decisions.

- **Career Resilience:** With a well-established personal brand, you're not just a job title—you're a recognized professional with a unique point of view. This makes you more adaptable to changes in the job market, as your reputation can help secure opportunities even during uncertain times.

## 2.   *Strategies to Build Your AI-Centric Personal Brand*

Here are practical steps to establish yourself as an AI-savvy product manager:

- **Create and Share Content:** Start writing blog posts or LinkedIn articles about your experiences with AI in product management. Share lessons learned from implementing AI in your projects, insights from AI certifications, or predictions about AI trends in your industry.

- **Engage in AI Communities:** Join AI-focused online communities, forums, or LinkedIn groups. Actively participate in discussions, share valuable resources, and connect with like-minded professionals.

- **Host Webinars or Workshops:** If you have deep insights into AI applications, consider hosting webinars or workshops. This positions you as a thought leader and allows you to engage with a broader audience interested in AI-driven product management.

- **Collaborate with AI Influencers:** Engage with AI thought leaders on social media, comment on their posts, and share their content. Building relationships with established AI influencers can boost your credibility and expose you to a wider network.

## 3.    *Using LinkedIn to Showcase Your AI Expertise*

LinkedIn is a powerful tool for personal branding, and leveraging it effectively can significantly enhance your career growth:

- **Optimize Your Profile:** Make sure your LinkedIn profile highlights your AI skills, certifications, and projects. Use a clear, professional headline like "AI-Focused Product Manager | Building Data-Driven Products."

- **Share AI Insights Regularly:** Post updates about AI trends, share interesting articles, or reflect on your own AI projects. Consistent sharing establishes you as an engaged, informed professional in the field.

- **Highlight AI Achievements in Your Experience Section:** If you've led an AI-driven project or implemented a machine learning model that improved user experience, be sure to detail these achievements in your LinkedIn experience section.

- **Get Endorsements and Recommendations:** Ask colleagues or managers to endorse your AI skills and provide recommendations that highlight your AI expertise. This adds credibility to your personal brand and makes your profile more attractive to potential employers.

## *Conclusion: Taking Charge of Your AI-Driven Career Growth*

Embracing AI as a product manager isn't just about staying relevant—it's about leading the charge in a rapidly changing industry. AI can help you make better decisions, create more personalized products, and stay ahead of market trends. By investing in AI certifications, actively building a personal brand, and continuously learning, you can position yourself as an indispensable asset in the tech landscape.

The next steps are up to you. Dive into AI courses, experiment with AI tools in your projects, and don't be afraid to share your journey. The future of product management is AI-driven—make sure you're not just part of it, but leading it.

 # What We Learnt

- **AI is a Career Booster:** Leveraging AI in product management helps you make smarter decisions, personalize user experiences, and predict user needs—all of which enhance your role and make you a standout in the job market.

- **AI Transforms Product Development:** AI speeds up ideation, automates design, and improves testing, making the product development cycle faster and more user-focused.

- **Certifications Matter:** Earning AI-related certifications (like Google's AI Product Manager or IBM's Applied AI Professional Certificate) builds your expertise, boosts your resume, and signals to employers that you're committed to growth.

- **Choosing the Right Certification:** Go for courses that are industry-recognized, align with your role, and match your learning style—this makes AI learning easier and more relevant.

- **Build Your Personal Brand:** Establish yourself as an AI-savvy product manager by sharing content, engaging in AI communities, and hosting events or webinars.

- **Leverage LinkedIn:** Use LinkedIn to showcase your AI skills, post about AI trends, highlight your projects, and get endorsements to strengthen your professional profile.

- **Be a Lifelong Learner:** AI is always evolving, so keep learning, experimenting, and sharing your insights. It's the key to staying ahead and leading in the AI-driven product management world.

# CHAPTER 12
## FUTURE-PROOFING YOUR CAREER WITH AI – ADAPTING, INNOVATING, AND LEADING THE WAY

Congratulations on making it to the final chapter! You've navigated through a whirlwind of concepts, strategies, and tools that are shaping the role of product management in an AI-driven world. By now, you've delved into how artificial intelligence is transforming everything from customer research and market analysis to roadmapping and user experience design. As we wrap things up, we'll reflect on the journey we've taken together, look ahead at the emerging trends, and talk about how you can continue to grow, adapt, and thrive as a product manager in this rapidly evolving landscape.

## 📖 Recap: What We've Learned and Why It Matters for You as a Future-Ready Product Manager

First, let's revisit the essential skills and insights we've explored throughout this book. Whether you're just stepping into product management or you're already seasoned in the field, each chapter has been packed with knowledge designed to build your confidence in leveraging AI to enhance your products, processes, and teams.

# 1. *Understanding AI as a Tool, Not a Threat:*

In the early chapters, we explored how AI is not here to replace you, but to complement and enhance your work as a product manager. You learned to view AI as a strategic partner that can help you make smarter decisions faster, allowing you to focus on the big picture – crafting products that not only meet user needs but anticipate them.

# 2. *The Power of AI in User Research and Data Analysis:*

Gone are the days of relying solely on traditional surveys and focus groups. We dived deep into how AI-driven tools can transform your approach to user research by analyzing large datasets, uncovering user behavior patterns, and predicting future trends. You now have the know-how to blend human intuition with machine-driven insights, making your products more user-centric than ever before.

# 3. *Roadmapping, Prioritization, and Decision-Making with AI:*

AI's predictive capabilities are particularly impactful in roadmapping and prioritization. You've learned to use AI-driven analytics to make more informed, data-backed decisions, improving your ability to pivot quickly in response to changing market demands. By integrating AI into your roadmap strategy, you can foresee obstacles, allocate resources more efficiently, and ensure your team is always focused on high-impact initiatives.

# 4. *AI in Cross-Functional Collaboration:*

We covered how AI can break down communication barriers within product teams. By automating routine tasks and providing data-driven insights, AI facilitates clearer communication between stakeholders, designers, developers, and marketers. You are now better equipped to foster a culture of collaboration, where AI assists in keeping everyone aligned on priorities and product vision.

## 5.    *Ethical AI and User Trust:*

No discussion of AI in product management would be complete without addressing ethics. As AI becomes more integral to product decisions, maintaining user trust becomes paramount. You learned about bias in AI algorithms, data privacy, and how to build transparency into your product's AI features. This ensures that your products are not only innovative but also responsible and user-centric.

Think of this recap as your handy toolkit—packed with skills and strategies to help you succeed. But remember, as they say, "What got you here won't get you there." Let's look at where AI and product management are headed in the future, and how you can keep pace – or better yet, lead the way.

## 📖 Looking Ahead: Future Trends in AI and Product Management You Need to Be Ready For

AI is an ever-evolving field that continues to push the boundaries of what's possible in product management[31]. Here are some of the most important trends you should be aware of as you gear up for the next phase of your career:

---

[31] https://www.visily.ai/blog/ai-trends-to-watch-for-product-management/

## 1. *Deep Learning and Enhanced Personalization:*

AI's potential for personalization is immense, and as deep learning models become more advanced, they will enable even more nuanced and individualized user experiences. Think about AI that doesn't just suggest products but anticipates needs before users even realize them. This kind of "hyper-personalization" is becoming the gold standard for user experiences, and as a product manager, you'll need to be adept at integrating these capabilities into your products without compromising privacy or user control.

## 2. *AI-Driven No-Code Platforms:*

The rise of no-code platforms has already started to democratize product development, and AI is only accelerating this trend. With AI-enhanced no-code tools, product managers will have even greater autonomy to create prototypes, run experiments, and test ideas without needing to rely solely on developers. This shift means that product managers will need to be both creative thinkers and proficient technologists, able to leverage no-code platforms to test hypotheses and rapidly iterate on ideas.

## 3. *AI in Strategic Decision-Making and Scenario Planning:*

AI is moving beyond operational tasks and into strategic roles. Imagine AI tools that can simulate different product strategies, helping you forecast potential outcomes based on varying market conditions, competitor moves, and user behaviors. These tools can provide you with a more comprehensive understanding of potential risks and rewards, allowing you to make strategic decisions with greater confidence and precision.

### 4.    *AI for Sustainability and Social Good:*

The next wave of AI innovation will emphasize sustainability and social responsibility. AI can help you design products that not only solve user problems but also address broader social issues like reducing carbon footprints, improving accessibility, and fostering inclusion. As a product manager, integrating these elements into your product vision will be essential for aligning with global trends and meeting user demands for socially conscious products.

### 5.    *The Rise of Explainable AI (XAI):*

One of the biggest challenges with AI is its "black box" nature. Users and stakeholders are increasingly demanding more transparency in AI-driven decisions. Explainable AI (XAI) aims to make AI systems more understandable to humans by providing clear explanations for how decisions are made. Product managers will need to champion XAI, ensuring that AI features in their products are transparent, accountable, and easy for users to understand.

These trends highlight just a few of the ways AI is reshaping the landscape of product management. Staying ahead of these changes requires not just awareness, but active engagement.

# 📖 Continuous Learning and Adaptation: Your Secret Weapon in a Rapidly Changing AI Landscape

If there's one takeaway from this book, it's this: the future belongs to product managers who never stop learning. AI is evolving at breakneck speed, and what works today might be outdated tomorrow. To remain relevant, here's what you should keep in mind:

# 1. *Stay Curious and Be a Lifelong Learner:*

The best product managers are the ones who are endlessly curious. Whether it's picking up a new programming language, diving into a different industry, or experimenting with the latest AI tools, a growth mindset is your biggest asset. Dedicate time each week to learning something new, whether it's a blog post, a podcast, or a hands-on experiment with a new AI tool.

# 2. *Build a Strong Network of AI Enthusiasts and Experts:*

Product management is a team sport, and the same goes for your learning journey. Surround yourself with people who are passionate about AI, whether through professional networks, online communities, or industry events. Engaging in conversations with AI experts can help you gain fresh perspectives, understand complex topics more deeply, and stay inspired.

# 3. *Experiment, Iterate, and Don't Be Afraid to Fail:*

The beauty of AI is that it's built on iteration and learning from data. Apply this principle to your career. Run experiments, test new ideas, and don't be afraid to fail fast. The more you experiment, the faster you'll learn what works and what doesn't. Remember, every failure is just another data point on your journey to mastery.

# 4. *Embrace Soft Skills as AI Takes Over Hard Skills:*

As AI takes over more technical and analytical tasks, soft skills like communication, empathy, and leadership will become even more critical for product managers. Focus on honing your ability to tell compelling stories with data, lead cross-functional teams with empathy, and inspire trust among users and stakeholders.

## 5.      *Be Adaptable – and Always Ready to Pivot:*

Change is the only constant in the world of AI. Be open to pivoting your strategy, changing your approach, and even learning new roles within the product management ecosystem. Flexibility and adaptability will not only help you manage AI-driven transformations but also allow you to lead them.

# Final Words: Embracing AI as Your Ally on the Road Ahead – It's Just the Beginning

As we draw this journey to a close, it's important to pause and reflect on the road we've traveled together. This book has aimed to be more than just a guide on AI's role in product management. It's been crafted as a *call to action*, a blueprint for embracing the next chapter of product development with excitement and a willingness to adapt.

But let's be clear: AI is not an endpoint or a silver bullet. It's not about having all the answers – it's about having the *right questions*. AI is a dynamic tool that's constantly evolving, and its value lies in how you choose to harness it, integrate it, and ultimately, lead with it. AI is here to *amplify* your capabilities, to *complement* your intuition, and to *elevate* your vision as a product manager. It's not here to define your role but to transform the impact you can have.

## 1. AI as the Catalyst, Not the Destination

Think of AI not as a destination but as a catalyst for innovation. It enables you to move faster, respond smarter, and think bigger than ever before. Whether it's refining user personas with machine learning algorithms, automating routine tasks to focus on strategic planning, or generating actionable insights from oceans of data, AI is the fuel that propels you forward. But it's up to you to steer the ship – to use AI thoughtfully, ethically, and creatively in shaping the products of tomorrow.

As AI becomes increasingly integrated into product workflows, it will change the way we define success. It will shift from simply delivering features to delivering *experiences* – ones that are more personalized, predictive, and in tune with user needs. AI will enable you to see opportunities where others see obstacles, to identify trends before they become mainstream, and to foster customer relationships that are not just transactional, but transformational.

## 2. Your Role in Shaping AI's Impact in Product Management

The beauty of AI in product management lies in its versatility, but with that versatility comes responsibility. As a product manager, you have a critical role in shaping AI's influence within your team, your product, and even your industry. You're not just adopting a tool – you're setting a precedent. By advocating for responsible AI, prioritizing user trust, and continuously testing and refining AI integrations, you'll become a leader who not only uses AI effectively but sets a high standard for how it should be implemented.

So, don't just aim to keep up with AI; aim to shape how it's used in your products. Be the one who defines what success with AI looks like, balancing the fine line between leveraging AI for speed and personalization, and maintaining the empathy and human connection that users still deeply crave. It's your job to make AI not just a feature, but a feature that *matters*. Make AI enhancements purposeful and aligned with your product's core mission.

### 3. Building a Career that Thrives on Change

This book isn't just about the now – it's about the *next*. Your career as a product manager will be defined not just by how well you adapt to AI but by how well you *embrace* the entire wave of technological advancements that come your way. AI, after all, is just one chapter in a much longer story of innovation in product management. Technologies like augmented reality, blockchain, and edge computing are just around the corner, promising new possibilities and new challenges.

The future of product management belongs to those who are comfortable with being uncomfortable – those who can step into uncharted territory, learn fast, and adapt quickly. It belongs to the product managers who are willing to go beyond their comfort zones and who never stop learning, whether through formal courses, industry events, podcasts, or simply by asking, "What's next?" Your curiosity will be your greatest asset, and your ability to adapt will be your competitive edge.

### 4. Embracing the Mindset of Continuous Reinvention

There's an old saying that goes, "If you're not moving forward, you're falling behind." In the AI era, this rings truer than ever. To be a successful AI-enabled product manager, you must embrace the mindset of continuous reinvention. It's not enough to be open to change; you need to *initiate* change. Whether it's adopting a new AI tool, rethinking a user journey based on predictive analytics, or transforming a team's workflow with automation, be the one who drives innovation forward.

Reinvention also extends to your skill set. The best product managers of the AI era will be those who understand not just how AI works but why it works, and how it can be aligned with broader business objectives. They'll be strategic thinkers who can evaluate the impact of AI from different angles – not just from a technical perspective but also from ethical, business, and user experience standpoints.

## 5. Lead with Empathy, even in a Data-Driven World

At the core of product management is a fundamental truth: it's all about the users. No matter how sophisticated AI becomes, the success of a product will still hinge on its ability to solve real user problems, meet actual needs, and create meaningful experiences. AI can offer you data, insights, and speed, but it's empathy that will allow you to truly understand your users and build products that resonate with them.

Remember, AI is a tool, but it's the *human element* that makes a product truly valuable. As AI helps you analyze user behavior and predict trends, use this information not to replace intuition but to enhance it. The most successful product managers will be those who can blend the art of empathy with the science of AI, ensuring that users feel heard, understood, and valued at every step of the journey.

## 6. Dare to Dream, Create, and Disrupt

The future of product management isn't just about keeping up with AI; it's about *owning* it. Dare to be bold, to experiment, and to push the boundaries of what AI can do for your products. When others see risks, see opportunities. When others focus on limitations, focus on potential. AI is not the limit; it's the launchpad.

It's not just about being a part of the AI revolution – it's about leading it. As you embark on your journey forward, dare to dream big, innovate relentlessly, and disrupt thoughtfully. The products you create have the power to not just meet user needs but to redefine what's possible.

In the end, the message is simple but profound: embrace AI, keep pushing boundaries, and be the one who drives change, not the one who gets driven by it. The future of product management is waiting, and it's more exciting, dynamic, and full of potential than ever. So, go ahead – be curious, be adaptable, and be fearless. Because the best product managers aren't the ones who know everything; they're the ones who are always eager to learn, experiment, and grow. The road ahead is long, but with AI as your ally, it's a road full of promise and possibility.

The world of product management is yours to shape. Make it count.

 ## What We Learnt

- **AI as a Tool, not a Threat**: AI complements product managers, helping make smarter, faster decisions and allowing focus on strategic, user-driven products.

- **AI in User Research & Data Analysis**: AI transforms user research by analyzing large datasets, identifying behavior patterns, and predicting trends for better, user-centric products.

- **AI for Roadmapping & Decision-Making**: AI's predictive capabilities enhance roadmapping, prioritization, and resource allocation, enabling quick pivots in changing markets.

- **AI in Cross-Functional Collaboration**: AI improves communication, automates routine tasks, and keeps teams aligned on product priorities and vision.

- **Ethical AI & User Trust**: Responsible AI usage is essential to maintaining user trust. Product managers should focus on transparency, accountability, and bias reduction in AI-driven products.

- **Deep Learning & Personalization**: AI will drive "hyper-personalization," anticipating user needs before they arise, requiring product managers to balance personalization with privacy.

- **AI-Driven No-Code Platforms**: No-code tools enhanced by AI enable faster prototyping, testing, and iteration, making product managers both creative thinkers and proficient technologists.

- **Strategic AI for Scenario Planning**: AI tools will aid in strategic planning by simulating potential outcomes, helping forecast risks and rewards for informed decision-making.

- **AI for Sustainability & Social Good**: AI will play a role in developing socially responsible products that tackle global challenges like accessibility, inclusion, and sustainability.

- **Explainable AI (XAI)**: As transparency becomes crucial, product managers must ensure AI features are clear, understandable, and user-friendly.

- **Continuous Learning & Adaptation**: To thrive in an AI-driven world, product managers need to embrace lifelong learning, build networks with AI experts, and be willing to experiment and iterate.

- **Soft Skills for AI Era**: As AI handles more technical tasks, communication, empathy, and leadership will be increasingly critical for effective product management.

- **Adaptability**: The key to success is adaptability—being ready to pivot strategies, change approaches, and explore new roles within product management as AI evolves.

# APPENDICES

# APPENDIX A: PRODUCT ROADMAPS

Product roadmaps serve as visual tools for aligning teams, setting timelines, and tracking development phases.

## Types of Roadmaps

**Feature Roadmap:** Provides a granular view of upcoming features.

- **Template Elements:** Feature name, release phase, priority (high/medium/low), expected delivery date, team lead, status (e.g., in progress, completed).

- **How to Use:** Use this roadmap to align engineering and design teams. Prioritize based on user needs, business impact, and development effort.

**Quarterly/Annual Roadmap:** Offers a high-level overview of major goals and milestones.

- **Template Elements:** Quarterly goals, major releases, strategic initiatives, dependencies, and risks.

- **How to Use:** Review with stakeholders during strategic planning sessions to ensure alignment across departments.

**Release Planning Sheet:** Focuses on short-term sprints and release cycles.

- **Template Elements:** Sprint name, backlog items, assigned team members, expected duration, risk assessment.

- **How to Use:** Use during sprint planning meetings to ensure clarity and trackability of deliverables. Include a column for user stories or feedback loops to ensure user-centric development.

## Advanced Roadmapping Tools

- **Tools like ProductPlan, Roadmunk, or Aha!** can be used to create dynamic, shareable roadmaps that allow for real-time updates.

- **AI-Enhanced Roadmapping:** Integrate AI tools that analyze historical project data, helping predict timelines, allocate resources efficiently, and identify potential delays.

# APPENDIX B: AI TOOLS CHECKLIST FOR PRODUCT MANAGERS

AI tools can enhance various stages of product management, from ideation to user feedback analysis. This checklist ensures the integration of relevant AI tools effectively.

## AI-Driven Market Research Tools

**Overview:** AI tools can assist in competitor analysis, user sentiment tracking, and trend prediction.

### *Tools to Include:*

- **Google Trends:** Tracks user interest over time.

- **IBM Watson Natural Language Understanding:** Analyzes sentiment in user feedback, reviews, and social media.

- **Sprinklr:** Monitors real-time social media mentions and sentiment.

**How to Use:** Integrate these tools into your early research phase to identify user pain points and emerging market trends. Use sentiment analysis to prioritize feature development based on customer needs.

# Predictive Analytics Platforms

**Tools like Tableau, Microsoft Azure AI, Salesforce Einstein** help forecast user behavior and identify engagement patterns.

**How to Use:** Leverage predictive analytics during the beta testing phase to identify feature adoption rates, churn risks, and user preferences. Use AI to segment users based on behavior, which allows for personalized product experiences and targeted marketing.

# Automation and Productivity Tools

**Overview:** Automate repetitive tasks to improve team efficiency.

**Recommended Tools:**

- **Zapier, UiPath, and Microsoft Power Automate** for integrating workflows across platforms.

- **Chatbot** Platforms **like Drift or Intercom:** Automate user interactions, customer support, and onboarding.

**How to Use:** Deploy these tools to streamline communication, gather user feedback, automate data analysis, and speed up decision-making processes.

## AI Implementation and Evaluation Checklist

- **Implementation Steps:** Define AI use cases, collaborate with data science teams, train models, conduct validation tests, and iterate based on feedback.
- **Evaluation Criteria:** Ensure AI solutions are accurate, reliable, and transparent. Include metrics like precision, recall, and user satisfaction in AI evaluations.

**How to Use:** Apply this checklist during AI implementation phases to ensure that ethical and performance standards are met consistently.

# APPENDIX C: DATA-DRIVEN DECISION-MAKING FRAMEWORKS

These frameworks help PMs leverage data effectively, ensuring decisions are grounded in user insights and predictive analytics.

## A/B Testing Framework

**Overview:** A/B testing helps optimize features by comparing user responses to different versions of a product.

- **Template Elements:** Hypothesis, control vs. variant details, metrics to track (e.g., conversion rate, bounce rate), results, insights, next steps.

**How to Use:** Use this framework during feature development to test new designs, user flows, and product elements. Ensure a sufficient sample size to achieve statistically significant results.

## User Behavior Analytics Dashboard

**Overview:** A dashboard for tracking real-time user engagement, conversion rates, and user journey insights.

- **Metrics to Include:** Daily active users (DAU), monthly active users (MAU), time spent on features, drop-off points, engagement rates.

**How to Use:** Use this dashboard to identify areas where users face friction, refine user journeys, and ensure feature adoption aligns with product goals. AI-powered analytics tools like Mixpanel,

Amplitude, or Heap can provide deeper insights by automatically clustering users based on behavior patterns.

## Predictive Analytics Overview

**Overview:** Predictive analytics helps forecast user trends, enabling PMs to plan features and product updates proactively.

- **Template Elements:** User segments, expected behavior changes, seasonality effects, marketing triggers, product development recommendations.

**How to Use:** Use AI-driven insights to predict user churn, recommend product features, or tailor user experiences based on forecasted needs. For example, use AI to predict user churn and trigger personalized messages or special offers to retain high-risk users.

# APPENDIX D: AI INTEGRATION PLAYBOOK

This playbook offers a step-by-step guide for integrating AI into various product management phases, from ideation to post-launch.

## Steps for AI Integration

- **AI Use Case Definition:** Identify specific use cases where AI can add value, such as automated customer support, real-time data analysis, or personalized recommendations.

- **Collaboration with AI Teams:** Collaborate with data scientists and engineers to select models, refine data inputs, and validate results.

- **Continuous Model Training:** Establish feedback loops for refining AI models based on user interactions and evolving data patterns.

**How to Use:** This playbook serves as a guide for launching new AI-powered features, ensuring they are user-centric and ethically sound.

## Ethical AI Checklist

**Overview:** Ensures AI-driven features comply with ethical standards.

- **Checklist Items:** Data privacy, bias detection, transparency in decision-making, user control options, and regular audits.

**How to Use:** Integrate this checklist during AI product development to ensure compliance with ethical guidelines and regulatory standards like GDPR or CCPA.

# Scenario Planning with AI

**Overview:** AI scenario planning involves using models to simulate different business environments and user responses.

- **Steps for Use:** Define key scenarios (e.g., user adoption under different marketing campaigns, economic changes, competitor responses). Use AI to simulate outcomes, prioritize responses, and adapt product strategies accordingly.

**How to Use:** Use scenario planning during strategic planning sessions to forecast market dynamics, refine roadmaps, and adapt to potential challenges.

# APPENDIX E: CROSS-FUNCTIONAL COLLABORATION TEMPLATES

Cross-functional alignment is crucial for product development success. These templates help PMs maintain clear communication and collaboration across teams.

## Cross-Functional Meeting Template

- **Template Elements:** Meeting agenda, roles, timelines, decision logs, follow-ups.

**How to Use:** Use this template for regular sync-ups with engineering, design, sales, and marketing teams. Clearly define responsibilities, track decisions, and ensure timely follow-ups on action items.

## Alignment Framework for AI Projects

**Overview:** Ensures all teams (e.g., AI developers, designers, marketing) are aligned on project goals and timelines.

- **Template Elements:** Project goals, AI use case specifics, target outcomes, role assignments, key milestones.

**How to Use:** Use this framework during AI project kick-off meetings to ensure alignment, clarify expectations, and set timelines.

# APPENDIX F: POST-LAUNCH EVALUATION TEMPLATES

These templates help PMs measure the success of AI-powered product features after launch.

## Success Metrics Dashboard

**Overview:** Tracks key metrics like user satisfaction, feature adoption rate, revenue impact, and return on investment (ROI).

- **Metrics to Include:** Feature usage rates, customer satisfaction scores (CSAT), net promoter score (NPS), conversion rates, revenue per user.

**How to Use:** Use this dashboard to regularly review feature performance and iterate based on user feedback. AI tools can assist by providing predictive insights into feature success.

## Post-Launch Retrospective Template

**Overview:** Analyzes the effectiveness of the AI implementation and the product launch.

- **Template Elements:** What worked well, what didn't, user feedback, data insights, areas for improvement, action items for the next iteration.

**How to Use:** Use this template during retrospective meetings to gather lessons learned, refine processes, and plan future launches more effectively.

# GLOSSARY

- **Agile Development**: An iterative approach to product management that focuses on collaboration, flexibility, and customer feedback.

- **Algorithm**: A set of instructions or rules designed for a computer to solve a problem or perform a task.

- **Artificial Intelligence (AI)**: The simulation of human intelligence processes by machines, especially computer systems.

- **A/B Testing**: A method of comparing two versions of a product or feature to determine which performs better.

- **Backlog**: A prioritized list of tasks, features, or improvements that are maintained and managed in the product development process.

- **Big Data**: Extremely large data sets that can be analyzed computationally to reveal patterns, trends, and associations.

- **Bug**: An error or flaw in software or hardware that causes a product to behave unexpectedly.

- **Chatbot**: An AI program designed to simulate conversation with human users, commonly used in customer service.

- **Continuous Integration**: A development practice where developers integrate code into a shared repository frequently.

- **Cross-Functional Team**: A group of people with diverse expertise working together towards a common goal.

- **Customer Journey Mapping**: A visual representation of the process a customer goes through to achieve a goal with a product.

- **Data-Driven Decision Making**: Making decisions based on data analysis and interpretation rather than intuition.

- **Deep Learning**: A subset of machine learning involving neural networks with many layers, used for more complex tasks.

- **Design Thinking**: A user-centric approach to problem-solving that emphasizes empathy, ideation, and experimentation.

- **Ethical AI**: The practice of designing, developing, and deploying AI systems in a way that aligns with ethical guidelines.

- **Feature Prioritization**: The process of deciding which product features to develop first based on customer needs, impact, and feasibility.

- **Iteration**: The repetition of a process to refine and improve a product.

- **Key Performance Indicators (KPIs)**: Quantifiable measures used to evaluate the success of a product or project.

- **Lean Product Development**: A methodology focused on creating value for users with minimal resources and maximizing efficiency.

- **Machine Learning**: A subset of AI where systems improve their performance over time without being explicitly programmed.

- **Minimum Viable Product (MVP)**: A product version with just enough features to satisfy early adopters and gather feedback for further development.

- **Natural Language Processing (NLP)**: The field of AI that focuses on the interaction between computers and humans through language.

- **Neural Network**: A set of algorithms designed to recognize patterns, inspired by the human brain.

- **No-Code Platforms**: Tools that allow users to create applications without traditional programming.

- **OKRs (Objectives and Key Results)**: A framework for setting and tracking objectives and their outcomes within an organization.

- **Predictive Analytics**: The use of data, statistical algorithms, and machine learning to identify future outcomes based on historical data.

- **Product Lifecycle**: The stages a product goes through, from ideation to growth, maturity, and eventual decline.

- **Product Roadmap**: A strategic plan that outlines the vision, goals, and progress of a product over time.

- **Regression Analysis**: A statistical method used to estimate relationships among variables, often used in data analytics.

- **Retrospective**: A meeting held after a product release to reflect on what went well and what can be improved.

- **Scalability**: The ability of a product or system to handle increased loads or expand without compromising performance.

- **Scrum**: An agile methodology that uses iterative cycles (sprints) for developing products.

- **Sprint**: A short, time-boxed period when a team works to complete specific tasks.

- **User Persona**: A semi-fictional representation of an ideal customer based on research and data.

- **User Story**: A simple, user-centered statement of a product feature or functionality, written from the user's perspective.

# RECOMMENDED READING & RESOURCES FOR CONTINUED LEARNING

## Books

- **"Lean AI: How Innovative Startups Use Artificial Intelligence to Grow"** by Lomit Patel – Offers insights on leveraging AI to scale products quickly, emphasizing lean practices in product development.

- **"The Art of Product Management with AI"** by Christopher Browne – Focuses on developing AI-driven product roadmaps and ethical AI strategies.

- **"AI for Product Managers: Building AI-Driven Products"** by Ritu Kapoor – Covers the essentials of AI in product management, from ideation to launch.

- **"AI Product Management: How to Build Products that Learn and Improve"** by Donald De Souza – Offers a detailed approach to developing adaptive AI products, emphasizing continuous learning and iteration.

- **"Product Roadmaps Relaunched: How to Set Direction while Embracing Uncertainty"** by C. Todd Lombardo, Bruce McCarthy, Evan Ryan, and Michael Connors – Explains modern roadmapping techniques, including AI-powered prioritization tools.

- **"AI-Powered Marketing: Strategies for AI-Driven Marketing Success"** by Katie King – While focused on marketing, it provides insights into product management for AI-powered customer experience.

- **"Artificial Intelligence for Business: A Roadmap for Product Managers and Executives"** by Doug Rose – A practical guide for PMs to understand AI's impact on business and product strategies.

- **"Designing Machine Learning Systems"** by Chip Huyen – Offers insights into designing AI systems and products, bridging the gap between AI development and product management.

- **"The AI-Powered Enterprise: Transforming Your Business with AI"** by Seth Earley – Focuses on AI strategies in product management, enhancing user experiences, and AI's role in decision-making.

## Online Communities & Networks

- **Mind the Product** - Offers blogs, forums, training, and global events for PMs.

  **Website:** mindtheproduct.com

- **Product Coalition** - A community-based platform with articles, meetups, and discussions on product management topics.

  **Website:** productcoalition.com

- **Product School** - Focuses on education and certification in product management, including AI for product managers.

  **Website:** productschool.com

# AI and Product Management Resources

- **Product-Led Alliance** - A community for product-led growth strategies, with resources on AI's role in product development.

  **Website:** productledalliance.com

- **AI Product Institute** - Dedicated to training PMs on building AI products.

  **Website:** aiproductinstitute.com

- **O'Reilly Media** - Features books and courses on AI in product management, like *"Designing Data-Driven Products"*.

  **Website:** oreilly.com

# Professional Organizations

- **Association of International Product Marketing & Management (AIPMM)** - Offers certifications like the Certified AI Product Manager (CAIPM).

  **Website:** aipmm.com

- **Product Management Institute (PMI)** - Provides training, resources, and a global network for product management professionals.

  **Website:** productmanagementinstitute.com

- **IEEE Product Safety Engineering Society (PSES)** - While more technical, it includes AI-focused safety aspects in product design.

  **Website:** ieee-pses.org

## Conferences & Events

- **ProductCon** - A conference run by Product School, which often includes AI and tech-oriented product management topics.

  **Website:** productschool.com/productcon

- **AI Summit** - Focuses on AI innovations, with some sessions dedicated to product management.

  **Website:** theaisummit.com

# ABOUT THE AUTHOR
## DIANA LEE

*Diana Lee is a transformative product leader with over 20 years of experience driving innovation across Fortune 500 companies and high-growth startups. Throughout her career, she has redefined how technology enhances financial services by creating solutions that are both sophisticated and accessible. As Head of Product at SigFig, Diana is at the forefront of leveraging AI and advanced technology to expand access to personalized financial tools.*

*Previously, she held key roles at Magnifi by TIFIN, Invesco, Parkside, and Taulia, where she led initiatives that fueled growth and enriched customer experiences. Known for her strategic vision and flawless execution, Diana has launched impactful products that set new industry standards.*

*Holding a bachelor's degree from UC Berkeley's Haas School of Business and an MBA from the University of Washington, Diana combines business insight with technical expertise. With a customer-first mindset, she leads high-performing teams that thrive on collaboration and operational excellence. Her forward-thinking approach to AI and innovative solutions empowers her to remain dedicated to redefining what's possible in FinTech, driving meaningful change for consumers everywhere.*

# ABOUT THE AUTHOR
## BALASUNDARAM SUBBUSUNDARAM

***Balasundaram Subbusundaram (Bala)*** *is a visionary FinTech leader with nearly two decades of experience delivering AI-powered financial solutions that set new industry standards. As Head of Product for Payments & Financial Services at Walmart Inc., a Fortune 1 company, he leads the development of embedded financial products and digital payment ecosystems that maximize customer lifetime value and operational efficiency.*

*Bala's career spans impactful roles at LendingClub, ESM Solutions, TurningTech, and Taulia (an SAP company). At LendingClub, he spearheaded the company's transformation into a neo-bank, expanding investment portfolios and enhancing borrower and investor engagement. His leadership on key projects has consistently driven business growth, operational stability, and market expansion, positioning him at the forefront of financial innovation.*

*In addition to his corporate success, Bala advises on Engineering Leadership at California State University, Chico, and supports the Transformational Leadership Program at Seton Hall University, helping shape future leaders. With advanced degrees from Syracuse and Anna University, he seamlessly integrates technical expertise with strategic foresight, fostering collaboration and innovation to position organizations for sustainable growth in a dynamic, competitive landscape.*